Walking With A Hero

26 LESSONS FOR CHILDREN'S CHURCH

by Ruth Powell

Illustrations by Steve Hayes

® STANDARD PUBLISHING

Cincinnati, Ohio   3375

Unless otherwise noted, Scripture quotations are from *The New International Version,* © 1973 by New York Bible Society International, © 1978 by New York International Bible Society (used by permission).

Table of Contents

Instructions

Elementary children can be thrilled and inspired by the life of the apostle Paul. They love stories of bravery and adventure and certainly Paul's life teemed with courageous action. Use the lessons in this series to help them walk with Paul and his companions. In Paul they will find a man worthy of example.

Parts of Lesson

Xamine

These notes about the Scripture text will help you in your personal study. A Bible dictionary, concordance, and Bible atlas will also help.

Xcite

These first minutes are important ones. They form a transition time between Bible school and theme of your program, so use the informality to your advantage. Establish a warm, friendly atmosphere. Sit on the floor if it is carpeted, or sit in a circle of chairs. Be ready to do something or ask a question as soon as the first child arrives, and then be flexible as the others come.

Some of your students see one another only during children's church. They may go to different schools during the week and study in different Bible-school classes. Use this time to build relationships. Greet visitors, help students learn one another's names, and let them tell what is happening in their lives: sad and happy events.

Follow up on the activities of the previous week; find out how attempts to apply the lesson went and listen to memory verses.

Preparation is important for the children to be able to participate successfully during worship. Select those children who will be helpers—read the Bible, pray, pass the offering plates. A teacher should explain the tasks and let the children rehearse if that is needed. Give instructions to the group for any special features.

Music is an important part of public worship. For it to be meaningful for your students, they must know the songs and understand them. Use this time to teach the songs suggested in the order of worship. You will recognize many of these songs as popular VBS songs.

If you do not have a pianist or guitarist to accompany your singing, get a musician to record the songs on cassette tape. If you are not comfortable

singing, you may want to record a vocalist singing the songs.

Xpress

Let this title be your weekly reminder that not only the leaders, but also the children must be worshiping. This is an opportunity for them to respond to God.

Order of Worship

All songs and Bible readings have been selected to correlate with the Bible story or theme. However, you may use the index on page 112 to select other songs, and concordance to select other Bible passages.

Several methods may be used for posting your order of worship for the day. It may be written on the chalkboard or flip chart; simple bulletins may be prepared.

A pocket chart (card holder) is a flexible tool. You may buy one at a school supply house that will hang on your front wall. Sentence strips are available, or you may cut your own 1¾" x 18" strips of lightweight posterboard. (If you have a carpenter or "handyman" in your congregation, he might be willing to build such a board. Pattern it after the Register of Attendance and Offerings or Hymns board. Make your strips to fit.) Print each song title on a strip. Also print on strips the words: *Prelude, Call to Worship, Bible Reading, Communion, Offering, Bible Story, Application Story,* and *Prayer.* These titles then may be inserted in the day's order into the proper slots of the pocket chart.

Introduction

An object lesson or a story is provided here to introduce the objective of the day's session. Use it to capture the students' interest.

Bible Story

The Bible story is your main feature. Make it as interesting and informative as you can. We have not provided the copy for your story; the Bible provides that! As you tell the story, use the audiovisual aids listed in the Related Products below. Remember that the boys and girls live in a media world; dry reading of the Bible text or a Bible story book will not reach them.

Application Story

These stories will help you apply the Scripture truths to the lives of your students.

Xpand

Xpand is the opportunity for the students to respond to the information they have been receiving.

Memorize

The psalmist said that he hid God's Word in his heart that he might not sin against God. That is good motivation for our helping our students do the same. Each lesson's memory verse relates to the theme, so that it is relevant to the study.

A shorter memory verse is sometimes suggested for the Primaries. If so, only the words in bold face type in the Scripture quotation are to be memorized by the Primaries.

To help you teach the memory verses, we suggest a method each week that will help the children learn that particular verse.

In the early lessons an alternative to the individual memory verses is suggested. Students may work on a longer passage over several weeks.

Apply

Next, the students expand their thinking by considering how to apply what they just heard. Quite often, a special activity is suggested for Primaries who are just beginning to read and write. When carrying out these application activities, keep alert for opportunities to guide conversation around the morning's topic.

Some lessons call for activity sheets that are provided on perforated sheets on pages 65 through 82. You have permission to remove these sheets and photocopy as many copies as you need for your students.

Products to Enrich Your Sessions

Pict-O-Graph Stories: *Early Life of Paul* (#2216) and *Later Life of Paul* (#2217), Standard Publishing: Cincinnati, Ohio. These flannelgraph figures will add life to the story.

Acts Map and Chart, Standard Publishing, #2668. Map shows Paul's journeys and the chart organizes the chronology of the events of Acts. This set is vital to these lessons.

Milliken Missionary Journeys of Paul, Milliken Publishing Co.: St. Louis, Missouri. Overhead transparencies.

Abingdon Lands of the Bible—New Testament, Abingdon: Nashville, Tennessee. Overhead transparencies.

Book of Acts Visualized, Gospel Services, Inc., P.O. Box 12302, Houston, Texas 77017. Filmstrips with records and manuals.

Life of Paul (885/886 and 887/888), Canon Bible Filmstrips, Double Sixteen Co., Wheaton, IL.

Life of Paul. Cathedral Films, P.O. Box 4029, Westlake Village, California 91359. Twelve black and white, thirty-minute films. A free preview film is available.

Paul, Standard Publishing, #2739. A Bible hero paperback.

The Man Who Saw the Light. Standard Publishing, #2418. Bible story book.

Double Trouble Puzzles—Acts of the Apostles, Standard Publishing, #2822.

Missions Unit

With all the study on the missionary trips of Paul, this is an ideal time to build an interest in the missionaries that your congregation supports. Write to one or two families. Request materials for a bulletin board display, slides, materials for the children, ideas of what your students can do to help the mission work, a prayer list, a report of their goals and plans, information about each family member, and a cassette tape or letter to the students.

Prepare an attractive display from the materials you receive. Get permission to send a few weeks' offering money to the missionary. If you do send the offerings, make a special chart to show the growing total. If the money will be used for a special project, make the chart relate to the project.

If any special mission emphasis is scheduled for the congregation during the twenty-six week study, ask planners to include your children's church program in some special way. The students might prepare a display, serve as ushers, or present special music. Invite the missionary to speak in children's church.

Memorizing Can Be Fun!

by Kit Lambeth

Do your pupils get excited over memorizing verses of Scripture? Chances are they don't—unless you've shown them it can be fun.

For years learning memory verses was considered work. It was something teachers assigned and pupils struggled with. Some churches even gave up and phased it out of their curriculum. Now, they see their mistake.

Why is it important to memorize Bible verses?

First, memorization is an effective learning tool. Second, when a child learns a truth by heart he is apt to use it in his daily life. Thus he becomes emotionally as well as intellectually involved. Third, memorization leads to understanding.

In the past, some teachers used memory work as an escape. As their pupils sat around a table, supplied with appropriate verses to be memorized, the teachers used the time to do other classroom chores. No wonder pupils hated memory work!

There is a better way. Good teachers realize that effective learning requires constant guidance of one sort or another, and a certain amount of preparation.

This is the key to making memory work fun. The secret to helping pupils learn Bible verses by heart is to saturate their learning time with the Holy Scriptures, repeatedly and in various ways.

The way in which you expose your students to the Scriptures makes a great deal of difference in how well they remember them. The methods you use can be as different as the children you teach, but they must always lead to understanding.

Encouraging children to memorize a group of words in a certain order is not the objective in Christian teaching. Students could memorize nursery rhymes just as easily and derive about as much meaning from them.

Learning memory work can, however, be both enjoyable and meaningful. Consider the following suggestions, which are adaptable to large or small groups:

1. Explain the words in a memory verse in simple language a child can understand. If he strays from the true meaning of the verse, repeat the verse with him. Spend extra time on difficult words.

2. Help pupils recall times when knowing a certain Bible verse would have helped them (when they were angry, afraid, sick, lonely).

3. Read or dramatize various situations that parallel with a verse of Scripture.

And here are some exciting ways to keep Bible verses before your pupils:

1. Display verses to be memorized in prominent places about the room.

2. Let pupils dramatize Bible verses, draw pictures of stick people obeying a verse, or set verses of Scripture to music. Allow students to compose their own melody.

3. Encourage pupils to incorporate Bible verses in their prayers.

4. Review memorized verses by playing games.

5. Display a large Bible where children can conveniently use it. Help them locate and read each verse for themselves.

We who teach must lay proper foundations for learning. It is much easier for young minds to learn a fact right the first time than to have to unlearn it later.

If we teach well the Scriptures our pupils are able to grasp, we do well. If we can help them to enjoy memorizing and learn from it, we do even better.

Adapted from *Key to Christian Education*, Spring, 1977. Standard Publishing.

Memorization Methods Used in This Book

Take-away words (flannelboard, slot chart, or magnet board).

Poster with thought segments on each line

Individual flash cards of the verses

Antiphonal recitation

Setting verses to music

Memory association techniques

Illustration

Mark or embellish the verse: underlining, arrows, capital letters, glow marks, circles, color variations, and print variety.

Memory verse puzzle

Speaking in unison

Key words on flash cards

Scrambled words on card with brads and yarn

Bible verse rebus

Make own memory cards

Mnemonic learning: topical, A-B-C letters, two ____ and 2 ____, alliterative, topical or storyline, parallels—like if you know ____ what? and if you do ____ what?

Words scrambled on cards

Bulletin Board Ideas

How do you use your bulletin board? Announce an event? Welcome new students? Promote the church library or youth group meetings? Teach new Bible words? Apply a lesson to everyday life? Stimulate interest? Develop an attitude? Provide review? Our designs will help you carry out several of those purposes.

Our first three suggestions are designed to help you either stimulate interest or review a lesson. For example, the "Whoooo" questions could challenge the students to listen for the answers in the morning's Bible story. Or, the questions could review the information learned in a lesson or several lessons. You can use "Do you know what happened in . . ." in a similar way.

Your students may get involved in making the display for "Where did Paul preach?" by drawing pictures to show all the various types of places he preached. Or, you could make it a progressive board by adding a picture in each lesson that Paul preaches in a new situation.

The last three designs are more general and can be prepared by the teacher or by the teacher with the children's help. They will help develop attitudes and apply general Biblical truths to life.

Plan now how you will make your bulletin board an important teaching tool during this study.

Enlarging a Pattern

You may want to enlarge these designs to help you make your boards. Here are three ways to do it.

1. Trace the pattern onto tracing paper or thin typing paper. Mark off this tracing with half-inch squares. Next, square off a piece of paper the size you wish the pattern to be. Number the squares the same way on both sheets. Place sheets next to each other and reproduce the design on the second sheet, one square at a time. Check the numbers for correct position.

2. Trace the pattern onto an overhead transparency. Project the transparency onto the paper or posterboard from which you will make the figure. Move the projector closer or farther away from the paper to get the size of image you want.

3. Place the book on an opaque projector. Project the image onto the paper or posterboard from which you will make the figure. Move the projector closer or farther away from the paper to get the size of image you want.

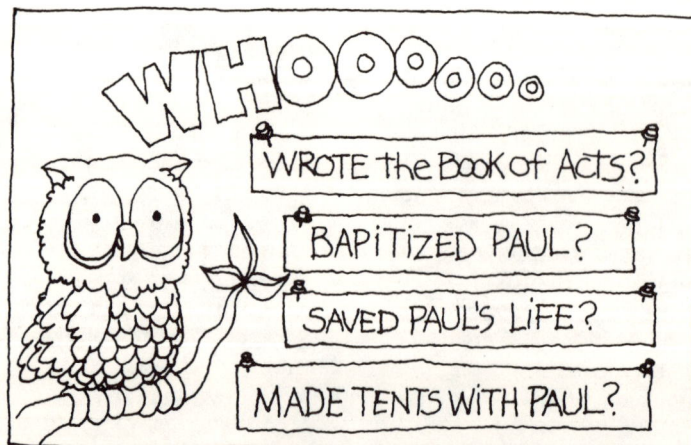

DO YOU KNOW WHAT HAPPENED IN...

JERUSALEM	BEREA	LYSTRA

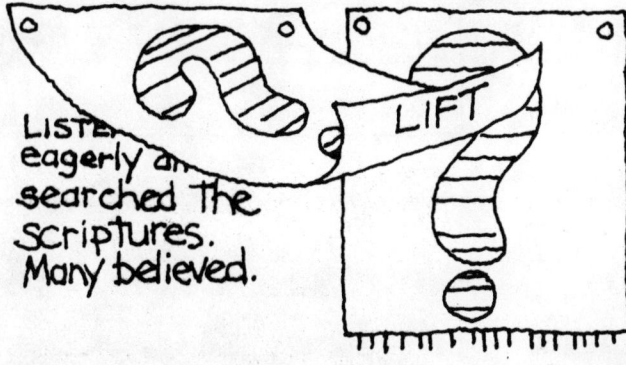
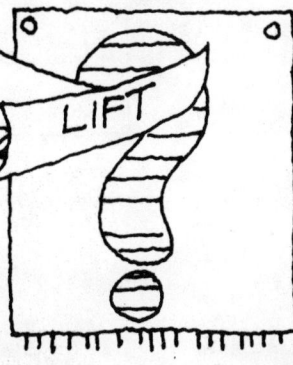

LISTE eagerly a searched the scriptures. Many believed.

LIFT

WHERE DID PAUL PREACH?

JAIL

SHIP

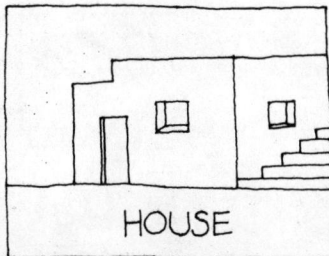

HOUSE

MARKET PLACE

WHAT CAN YOU DO WITH YOUR HANDS?

ALL CHILDREN LOVE JESUS IN THE SAME LANGUAGE

CHRISTIANS COME FROM ALL WALKS OF LIFE.

Lesson One
Acts 6:8—8:1

Xamine

Acts 6:8. Stephen was one of seven young men appointed to help in caring for poor widows of the congregation in Jerusalem.

6:9. Stephen was a Greek and evidently worshipped in a synagogue where the Greek language was spoken.

6:15. Note the similarity to Moses' face when he came down after spending time with God.

7:2-50. This is a beautiful defense, not of himself, but of Christ.

7:51-53. He gives a stern rebuke to self-righteous men.

7:54-60. What a story of death and triumph!

7:58—8:1. We meet Saul of Tarsus, a sincere man, but one who was wrong.

Xcite

While the rest of the arriving students play the game and learn the songs, one teacher should select and rehearse students to read the call to worship, serve as ushers, and offer prayer.

Play the simple game, *The Lost Child,* to help students become more aware of one another's presence. If they don't know one another's names, wear name tags for a few weeks.

Send one child from the room. Select a child to hide while the others change seats. (If new children arrive during the hiding, their presence will just add to the challenge.) Call the first child back into the room to tell which player is hiding. If he is able to tell, choose another child to be *it*.

Teach the songs, "We Praise Thy Name," page 83, and "We Gather Together," page 97, if your students don't know them. Point out that both songs are speaking to God directly; urge them to sing them accordingly.

Xpress

Order of Worship

Prelude
Call to Worship: Psalm 100:1, 2
"We Gather Together," 97
"We Praise Thy Name," 83
"Jesus Loves Me"
Communion
Offering
Introduction/Bible Story
Application Story
Prayer

Introduction

Bring two or three small to medium-sized rocks to class.

Can you think of some uses for rocks? Allow discussion. *Some are used for making walls, houses, walkways, and rock gardens. Of course there are destructive uses for rocks: breaking windows, fighting, and throwing with the intent to hurt someone.*

Now it is very likely that you boys and girls are not rock-throwers. You would not try to cripple an animal or injure a person with a rock. You know better than to throw rocks at windows or street-lights.

The person in our story today was not a rock-thrower either, but he stood by and watched without protest, while others threw. In today's lesson we're going to see how a rock, like one of these, can make a brave person out of you.

Bible Story

Tell this account as an introduction to the life of Paul (Saul). This tragic episode was to overshadow much of his life.

Application Story

Jimmy was never able to forget that day. He and his friends were down by the creek skipping rocks when a mangy, unattractive mongrel dog came down to get a drink. One of the boys shouted, "Hey, get out of here, you dirty old dog," and tossed a pebble at the pup. It struck the dog on the hind leg; he jumped sideways, giving a shrill, funny-sounding yip. The boys laughed and ringed around the frightened animal, tossing rocks at it mercilessly. Jimmy didn't throw any rocks. He just watched. Yet that cruel scene came again and again to torment him. He knew that he had been a coward because he hadn't even tried to defend the little dog.

Paul, or Saul of Tarsus as he was known then, was never able to forget the day he had watched the brave young Christian, Stephen, stoned to death. He recalled again and again how he had stood by and consented to Stephen's death.

How about you? Do you speak up to protest against cruelty (hurting, teasing, telling lies about someone)? Or, do you remain silent even though you disapprove?

A rock can make a brave person out of you—if you speak up and tell others that it is wrong to throw it.

Xpand

Memorize

If you have not yet read the article, Memorizing Can Be Fun! in the introductory pages, do that now.

Today's Verse
"Anyone, then, who knows the good he ought to do and doesn't do it, sins."

James 4:17

Print the verse on the chalkboard with its reference. Discuss what actions the students would know to do, but might not do.

Primaries: Select volunteers to come up and act out such an example. Have the rest of the children recite the verse and reference during the action. For example, a child drops a tray of food in the cafeteria. Another child walks by without helping. After several pantomimes, the students will know the verse.

Middlers/Juniors: Ask the group to read the verse together two or three times, trying to remember it. Instruct students to close their eyes and try to visualize the verse. While their eyes are closed, remove two words. Then ask the group to open eyes and read the verse again, filling in the missing words. Repeat the process until all words are removed and only the Bible reference remains. Ask several pupils to recite the verse from memory.

Memory Project
"The earth is the Lord's and everything in it,
  the world, and all who live in it;
for he founded it upon the seas
  and established it upon the waters.
Who may ascend the hill of the Lord?
  Who may stand in his holy place?
He who has clean hands and a pure heart,
  who does not lift up his soul to an idol
  or swear by what is false.
He will receive blessing from the Lord
  and vindication from God his Savior.
Such is the generation of those who seek him,
  who seek your face, O God of Jacob."

Psalm 24:1-6

If you have elected to guide your pupils in memorizing the longer passages rather than the individual verses, begin with this one that describes our great God. As you and the children memorize, guide them in discussing ways it relates to these first lessons.

If the passage is being memorized by the children as an extra project, try to discuss briefly with them the application to the lessons, either as they work or when they recite the passage for credit.

When several students know the passage, invite them to recite it as a group or individually during the worship time.

Apply

From the ideas suggested by the children during the discussion of James 4:17, select situations that require courage to do what is right. For example, the lunch tray incident may call for courage for a boy who might be teased if he helped a girl. (Be ready with some examples if needed.)

Let small groups determine how the child might do the action that is "good" in a case; then volunteers practice carrying out the action.

Lesson Two

Acts 9:1-19

Xamine

Acts 9:1, 2. Verse one is a continuation of the story from Acts 8:1-3. Saul, fired with zeal and evidently goaded by a guilty conscience (see Acts 26:14), has now become a man dedicated to finding, arresting, and punishing followers of the Way.

9:2, 3. Jerusalem to Damascus is about 150 miles northeast, so it was a long difficult journey in those times. The Way is a specific term used to describe the Christian faith and life.

9:4. In Acts 26:14 we read that all fell to the ground.

9:5, 6. Saul knew that the voice came from heaven, but he did not know that it was Jesus until Jesus identified Himself.

9:7. From Acts 22:9 we learn that they saw the light and heard the sound, but only Saul understood the words.

9:10-16. Ananias, afraid to go to Saul, is given firm and direct instructions as to where to go and what to say. Paul and Ananias are introduced to each other in the same way—a vision.

9:17-18. Depending fully on Christ's word, Ananias put himself in a position where he would be helpless if Saul wanted to take him.

9:19. Saul put his submission to Christ ahead of his own comfort, for he obeyed Him in baptism before he ate and was strengthened.

Xcite

A game of *Simon Says* will introduce today's theme and also get rid of the children's wiggles so that they can better worship. When you introduce the game, emphasize the importance of listening carefully and following directions.

Teach the song, "Happiness," page 83, for use during worship.

Xpress

Order of Worship

Prelude
Call to Worship: Psalm 105:4

"We Praise Thy Name," 83
"Happiness," 83
"Jesus Loves Me"
Communion
Offering
Introduction/Bible Story
Application Story
Prayer

Introduction

Make three signs saying, *Detour, Stop,* and *Slow.* Show these at the appropriate times as you talk to the class.

Road signs are warning signals that we can't ignore if we want to have a safe journey. If we refuse to heed the sign that says Detour and go straight ahead, we will find ourselves in trouble, perhaps in a ditch or a mud hole. When a sign says Slow, there is a good reason. There may be a dangerous curve or a rough road ahead. The Stop sign means just what it says. STOP. You may have come to a crossroad. Maybe there is a train coming. Perhaps a bridge is out. Whatever the reason, it is necessary to stop.

Paul had to come to a stop in his road. He did not ignore the sign he received and his whole life direction was changed. Paul knew that the most important directions of all come from God.

God has given us directions and warnings, too. We need to be alert to see and know God's directions for our lives, for He knows what lies ahead and what our paths should be.

Bible Story

This is an exciting story. Help the children to understand that Saul was trying to do what was right when he was persecuting the Christians. He thought the followers of Christ were enemies of God. Jesus looked at Saul's heart and knew that this was a man whom He could use.

When Saul finally understood that in order to serve God truly, he must accept and serve Christ, Saul was willing to turn his whole life around.

Proud Saul, a Pharisee, a leader, is led helpless and blind into the city where he must wait humbly to be told what he should do. He knows he has been terribly wrong but he doesn't know how to make it right.

Imagine Ananias' dilemma. This man Saul is dangerous, a persecutor. Ananias doesn't want to go and stand before him and preach him a sermon! But he goes, because the Lord tells him to go.

Saul must have been relieved to receive his sight. Yet even greater joy came in knowing that the Lord was willing to forgive him and accept him.

Application Story

His feet were getting so sore that he was afraid he couldn't walk much farther. He was so tired, too. Wishing that he had never come on this long-awaited camping trip, Jim sat down on a mossy log. If only he'd stayed with the group as he was supposed to do. He hadn't meant to go so far when he'd followed the little fawn from the edge of the campground. He had been sure that he knew the way back to camp. As he sat in exhaustion, he rubbed absently at the soft moss on the side of the log.

"I'm going to give it another try," he said to himself. "I just know camp is in that direction."

Pushing on as bravely as he could through the deep woods, he walked for some time until he realized he was back at the log where he'd rested. He'd heard of lost people going in circles—and he seemed to be doing it too. He sank down and rested his head against the mossy log.

Suddenly a lesson he had read last year came to his mind. In science class he had learned something about directions, fungus, and the north. Didn't fungus grow more on the north side of trees in certain parts of the country? The moss had reminded him, for some types of moss were really fungi.

Getting to his feet, he began checking the trunks of trees. Sure enough, the fungal growth was heavier on one side. He had wandered from the south side of the camp, so now he knew a direction to walk. With renewed deteroination he began walking, making marks with his knife on the trees and rocks as he passed. Before very long he came to a stream; he felt pretty sure that it was the one that ran through the camp. He joyfully followed it upstream and, to his great relief, after about ten minutes he heard and answered the anxious voices calling his name. He took a few moments right then to thank God for helping him to find the right path.

Jim had been so sure that he was right while he had wandered farther and farther away in the wrong direction.

Saul was going the wrong way on that road to Damascus. Oh, it was the right road to Damascus, but Saul wasn't going the right way. For he wasn't going Jesus' way; he was going Saul's way. He wanted to do right, but he was doing wrong.

After the Lord spoke to Saul, Saul could have refused to listen. Blind and angry, he could have gone on into Damascus and fought against Christ. But he didn't.

Let's all be willing to hear the voice of the Lord when He speaks to us through His Word, and let's be willing to stop and change our direction and go in the way that God wants us to go. He knows the right path for each of us. Let's follow Him.

Xpand

Memorize

Today's Verse
"In all your ways acknowledge him,
   and he will make your paths straight."
                              Proverbs 3:6
Explain carefully the word "acknowledge" and discuss the verse with the children. This verse fits the tune of "Here We Go 'Round the Mulberry Bush" with an emphasis on this new word that should help the children remember it.

"In all your ways acknowledge him,
   acknowledge him, acknowledge him,
In all your ways acknowledge him,
   and he will make your paths straight."
After singing the verse to the tune several times, students should soon be able to recite without the music.

Memory Project
Continue work on Psalm 24:1-6.

Apply

Primaries: Prepare as a choir to sing during next Sunday's worship the song, "Beyond Jerusalem."

Do you remember in what city Stephen lived? (Jerusalem) *Yes, Jerusalem was the city where the church began. Listen as I sing a song and tell me what the singers are going to do.* Sing "Beyond Jerusalem." Discuss. Explain that Judea was the area in which Jerusalem was located. Compare to your town and state.

After the children know the words add expression to the singing of the words.

Middlers/Juniors: Today's puzzle will provide a good review of the facts in today's Bible account. The puzzle is printed on page 65, ready to use. Tear it out and photocopy the number of puzzles you need. Note: do *not* lose the original because the puzzle for lesson four is on the back of the puzzle.

When properly answered, the boxes spell the name of Paul's destination—Damascus, Syria.

Lesson Three
Acts 9:19-31

Xamine

Acts 9:19, 20. Having completed his obedience to Christ, he is strengthened by the "meat" or food he takes. Once strengthened, he began on the mission to which he would dedicate the rest of his life.
9:21. It is not surprising that his hearers were amazed, for they had known of Saul's intention to arrest the followers of Christ. From Galatians 1:15-18 we learn that Saul went to Arabia for some time, and then returned to Damascus. The many days added up to about three years.
9:24, 25. Probably the basket was a large food basket and it could have been lowered from the window of one of the houses that overhung the city wall in an unguarded section.
9:26-28. Barnabas, who would later travel with Saul, believed that Saul was sincere and took him to Peter and James (Galatians 1:18-19) and Saul was at last accepted among the believers.
9:29, 30. The Grecians were the same ones who led the opposition to Stephen.
9:31. There followed a time of rest from persecution for the churches, a time when they were able to grow in number and in spirit.

Xcite

As students arrive assign them to groups of four, ensuring that each group has an older student who can write. The members of each group should list facts about one of them on a piece of paper. When most groups are ready, let someone from a group read its list to the rest of the students who try to guess the identity of the person being described.

Teach the song, "Down the Damascus Wall," page 87, explaining that it describes part of this morning's Bible story.

Xpress

Order of Worship

Prelude
"We Gather Together," 97
Call to Worship: James 4:8a
"We Praise Thy Name," 83
"Happiness," 83
"Jesus Loves Me"
Communion
Offering
Introduction/Bible Story
Application Story
"Down the Damascus Wall," 87
"Beyond Jerusalem" by choir
Prayer

Introduction

Take a packet of seeds to class and pour a few of the seeds into your hand. Don't let anyone see the label.

This little seed doesn't look like much, does it? It certainly isn't impressive. Yet it has great possibilities. In order to prove this, though, you have to plant it, don't you? Now maybe you think it is a flower seed—and you think it might be lettuce. Well, I believe that it is a _____ seed. At least that is what the packet says that it is. Show packet. *How can this little seed prove finally, once and for all, what it is? It must grow. Plant it and give it time and care and it will show itself for just what it is.*

Saul wasn't trusted when he was first a Christian. The Christians were still afraid of him and the Jews felt that he had betrayed them and their cause. He was like this seed. Only time was going to prove whether he was worth anything at all.

Like Saul, all we can say about how good we are going to be does not prove what we are. Yet, like this seed, we too will become wonderful examples of what God can do.

Bible Story

In two cities the newly converted Saul of Tarsus meets with amazement and angry rejection. It must have taken a great deal of courage to stand first before the Jews in Damascus, then before the Christians in Jerusalem. Yet Saul is as determined to preach and to teach for Jesus as he once had been determined to arrest believers.

Application Story

James must change schools in the middle of his eighth-grade year. He had been attending Winslow

Junior High, but now that their apartment building was being torn down the family had to move. Mom and Dad were excited to be buying a place of their own across town.

James was an excellent baseball player. He had been a well-known and important man on Winslow School's team. He loved to play and played well. Now he wanted to play on the new school's team. He felt pretty confident that the team would be glad to have a player like him. But to his amazement and disappointment, he wasn't wanted at all, at least not for this year. The new team was afraid that James' loyalty and team spirit were still back at Winslow. He would have to wait and prove that he was loyal to the new school.

James, like Saul, knew some sad and difficult days. Both knew that only time and their own actions would prove that they were to be trusted.

Xpand

Memorize

Today's Verse

"**Watch out for false prophets. They come to you in sheep's clothing, but inwardly they are ferocious wolves.** By their fruit you will recognize them. Do people pick grapes from thornbushes, or figs from thistles?"

Matthew 7:15, 16

The first verse is all that most **Primaries** can learn. First graders may even be limited to the first sentence.

Explain false prophets, thornbushes, thistles, and how one can judge the fruit of a teacher. (Use the Christians' judging of Paul's teaching as an illustration.) This is a good opportunity to stress the importance of studying the Bible to see if what a teacher or preacher says can be found there.

Make a poster of the pictures that illustrate key words in the verses. It will help the students memorize more easily.

Memory Project

Are you allowing a time during the morning's schedule for children to recite what they are memorizing? Are any of the children ready to recite the passage as part of next Sunday's worship service?

Apply

Primaries: Make copies of the Find-the-Words Puzzle on page 67. It will be an excellent reinforcement of the memory verse. Early finishers can color the pictures. Recite the verse together.

Middler/Juniors. Help your students get acquainted with the places mentioned in these first lessons.

Distribute to the students the maps you photocopied from the map on page 68. Instruct them to write their names on their maps; collect them at the end of the session to hold for further work.

As you carry out these map activities, it will be more beneficial to the students if you point to the locations on a large map. We highly recommend the map in Acts Map and Chart (#2668, Standard Publishing). Or, make an overhead transparency of the student map and project it.

For two or three minutes let children name a country, city, or water title that they recognize. Teach them to use the letter/number coordinates around the edge of the map to find places named.

In what city was Stephen stoned? Have all students point to Jerusalem. *In what city was Paul baptized?* Locate Damascus. *Where did Paul go soon after his conversion?* Explain that Arabia extends up northeast from the title on the student map. Show the purple area on the map from the Acts set. *Where did some Jerusalem Christians take Saul?* Help them find Caesarea. *Where did they send him and why to that city?* Guide them further north to his hometown, Tarsus.

Distribute colored pencils or fine-tipped markers. Tell students to select a color to draw Paul's route from Jerusalem to Damascus into Arabia back to Damascus to Jerusalem to Caesarea to Tarsus. Draw such a route on your wall map or overhead transparency. If you are using the Standard wall map, a light line shows a route for you to follow as far as Jerusalem. You will be on your own to draw the line to Caesarea and Tarsus. The *Standard Bible Atlas* shows the route on map 15, page 23.

To be able to erase the colored routes for future use of the map, mount the map on poster board and cover it with clear Con-Tact paper. Nonpermanent marker lines will then wipe off easily.

Lesson Four

Acts 11:19-30; 12:25

Xamine

Acts 11:19. This verse begins a whole new direction for the Acts of the Apostles. Primarily the story thus far has dealt with the gospel being presented to the Jews. Even though the Christians had been scattered far and wide, at first they carried the message of Christ only to the Jews whom they found in their new locations. From this point, the story shifts to the way in which the message of Christ is carried to the Gentile world.

11:20. Cyrene was a city of Northern Africa. These Jews spoke the Greek language and evidently spoke not just to Greek-speaking Jews, but to Gentiles as well.

11:21-24. The Church at Jerusalem was concerned. Interested and ready to send help, the church sent Barnabas to Antioch to observe this work and perhaps determine whether or not it was acceptable that these Gentiles were turning to Christ.

11:25. Barnabas had not forgotten Saul and now, with the work in Antioch growing and flourishing, he makes the journey up to Tarsus to find Saul and bring him back.

11:26. A new name for the disciples came into use. It might have been chosen by the Gentile believers themselves or it might have been applied to them by the unbelievers.

11:27-30. Agabus appears again much later in Saul's life, but here, he and the other prophets warn of hard times coming.

Xcite

If you are teaching this lesson during the winter where there is snow, take the group outside to make a snowball. Or, post pictures of snow scenes around the room for a picture walk.

Teach the song, "We Will Go to All the World," 110. Relate its words to the evangelizing of the early Christians.

Xpress

Order of Worship

Prelude
Call to Worship: Isaiah 25:1

"We Praise Thy Name," 83
"Happiness," 83
"Jesus Loves Me"
Communion
Offering
"Beyond Jerusalem," Primary Choir
Introduction/Bible Story
Application Story
"We Will Go to All the World," 110

Introduction

Have you ever rolled a snowball down a hill? What happened? The snowball grew, didn't it? As it rolled along over the soft snow, other snow stuck to it and it grew and grew. The farther it rolled, the bigger it grew. That's the way snow is: it compacts and clings and keeps right on growing as it goes.

That is somewhat the way it was with the early church. As it moved, it grew. The early Christians went out from Jerusalem, driven out by the persecution there, and everywhere they went, they attracted other people to become Christians like themselves. They did not leave Christ behind in Jerusalem. They had taken Him into their lives and He was with them. As they met new people in new places, they shared what Jesus had done for them. Like the snowball, wherever the Christians went, others came to join with them in faith; the farther away they scattered, the more others came to know about Jesus as the Son of God.

Bible Story

This lesson is more informational than most. Reintroduce the class to Barnabas. Remind them of how he had taken Saul's part when the church in Jerusalem had been afraid Saul was still their enemy. Bring Saul back into the story as he is called to come and help in this thriving new congregation in Antioch.

These verses help us to see just how it was that Saul, an ardent Jew, came to begin to work with and understand the Gentiles. God was working in Saul's life and preparing him for the great adventure that was to begin very soon. Saul will go out from Antioch to carry the story of Jesus as no one had done before.

It is important in studying this lesson to sense the excitement of the early Christians. What seemed like a great misfortune to the church in Jerusalem was really a great blessing. The church grew because it had to scatter abroad. Yet if these Christians had not been willing to share the gospel wherever they went, there would have been no such growth. It was this desire to tell others about Christ and His love that caused the church to grow, not only reaching the Jews with whom they came in contact, but reaching out to the Gentile world as well.

Application Story

Have you ever had really good and exciting news to tell? Mary had. She was going on a long train trip by herself to spend two whole weeks on her aunt and uncle's farm. She was so happy about this prospect that she told everyone she saw. She told the mailman when he delivered the mail, the checkout girl at the supermarket, and a stranger who was walking her dog.

Mary could hardly wait to get to school so she could tell her friends. As soon as she reached school her teacher knew that Mary had some happy news to share. She could tell just by looking at her face. She had a big smile and her eyes were shining. It wasn't long before the whole class knew about Mary's exciting plans and was able to be happy with her.

The early Christians were like Mary. They were so filled with the good news about Jesus that wherever they went, they told others. Those Jews back in Jerusalem who had thought that they would destroy the church by persecuting the Christians and making them scatter out of the city found that they had just helped Christianity to grow—out into the towns and cities across the world of that day.

Xpand

Memorize

Today's Verse

"Therefore go and make disciples of all nations, baptizing them in the name of the Father and of the Son and of the Holy Spirit, and teaching them to obey everything I have commanded you."

Matthew 28:19, 20a

This passage can be learned with a mnemonic method. Show the students that there are three questions (two for Primaries) that could be asked about this sentence. "Go and do what?" "Doing what?" "And doing what?" Tell them that you will ask a question to which they will answer a part of the verse.

Teacher: "Therefore go and do what?" Students: "Make disciples." Teacher: "Make disciples doing what?" Students: "Baptizing them." Teacher: "And doing what?" Students: "Teaching them." Repeat the series of questions and answers several times.

When the students have learned the basic answers to the questions, they simply add the rest of the phrases as they answer the questions. Teacher: "Therefore go and do what?" Students: "Make disciples of all nations." Teacher: "Doing what?" Students: "Baptizing them in the name of the Father and of the Son and of the Holy Spirit." Teacher: "And doing what?" Students: "And teaching them to obey everything I have commanded you."

After working through the pattern of questions and answers several times, let the students recite the sentence several times without the questions.

Memory Project
Psalm 24:1-6;   This is the last Sunday for this passage. If no one has yet recited it as a call to worship, select an individual or group to do this next week.

Apply

Primaries: In the application story today Mary was excited about her good news. Many of your students may have some news to tell also. Use this time to let your Primaries take turns telling of something good that happened during the last week or two. Start the sharing with some news of your own; your example will help them understand the assignment. To be sure that everyone gets an opportunity to talk, use a timer. For example, if you have fifteen minutes for ten students, allow just one-and-a-half minutes.

Middlers/Juniors: Spend a few minutes letting the students add today's movements of Saul to their maps. If they have more than five color choices in their pencils, allow them to select a color different from that used last week. Guide them in drawing a line from Tarsus to Antioch to Jerusalem. For the journey back to Antioch instruct students to draw a set of arrows pointing each way on the one line.

As the children complete their map work, distribute copies of the questions and code on page 66 so that they may test themselves on their recall of the events of today's study.

Answers: 1. *Barnabas* was sent to Antioch to visit the church. 2. Barnabas traveled to *Tarsus* to get Saul to help him. 3. Saul and Barnabas worked in the church in *Antioch* together. 4. The disciples were first called *Christians* in Antioch. 5. Agabus came up from *Jerusalem.* 6. The Christians in Antioch sent help to the people in Judea where a *famine* was coming.

Lesson Five
Acts 13:1-12

Xamine

Acts 13:1, 2. Verse one names five men who were working as ministers to the church in Antioch. Little is known about the other three beyond what is stated, but in verse two, the Holy Spirit instructed them to separate Barnabas and Saul and set them apart for a very special task. The solemnity of the occasion made prayer with fasting appropriate.

13:4. Note that the one doing the sending is the Holy Spirit. Seleucia is the seaport, at the mouth of a river, from which they set sail for the island of Cyprus. In going there, Barnabas was approaching his own people (Acts 4:36).

13:5. Landing on Cyprus at the chief city of Salamis, they first went to the synagogue to preach to the Jews living there. This would be their practice everywhere. John Mark is introduced as their travelling companion.

13:6-8. Bar-Jesus, or Elymas, is a false prophet, a magician. The name means son of Jesus (Greek form of Joshua). He had considerable influence on the deputy of the country, Sergius Paulus.

13:9-11. These verses contain a startling miracle as Saul (who now begins to be known as Paul) rebukes Bar-Jesus. The punishment was not Paul's vengeance, but God's warning.

13:12. It was evident that Paul represented a power superior to all of Elymas' magic. Having seen this and listened to Paul's message, Sergius Paulus believed.

Xcite

If you have the time and space, a game of *Blindman's Bluff* will introduce one aspect of today's lesson.

A quieter adaptation will not only introduce the theme, but also help the children concentrate better on getting to know one another's voices. Blindfold a volunteer. Invite another volunteer to say a few words or sentences. The blindfolded person must then identify the voice.

Teach the song, "Jesus Died for Men," 90. Discuss its meaning and application to the communion service.

Xpress

Order of Worship

Prelude
Call to Worship: Psalm 46:10a or Psalm 24:106
"We Praise Thy Name," 83
"Happiness," 83
"Jesus Died for Men," 90
Communion
Offering
Introduction/Bible Story
Application Story
"We Will Go to All the World," 110

Introduction

Obtain a picture of a blind person, a book of braille, or some symbol of blindness. Also use the blindfold from the opening game.

There is an old saying, "There is none so blind as he who will not see." Blindness is a severe handicap but, like most handicaps, it can be overcome. The blind person can train him or herself in order to get along quite well, learning to read books written in braille, learning to function safely and well in the world of seeing people. Yet even with these possibilities, no one would choose to be blind—at least not physically. But there are people who refuse to see, who do not want to see what is real and true and good. These people are like ones who blindfold themselves. Bar-Jesus was like this. He did not want to see and understand the truths being taught by Saul and Barnabas. He refused to see and so, for a time, he was struck blind.

Bible Story

Picture this scene clearly. Paul and Barnabas are on the island of Cyprus and they are very glad to have the opportunity of speaking to the ruler of the island. Bar-Jesus is using whatever means he has to distract Sergius Paulus from receiving the message of Christ, arguing and disputing with Paul in order to turn the deputy away.

Help the class to realize that Paul was not just trying to get even with the magician for interrupting. He was determined that none should hinder the message of Christ.

Application Story

A large earthquake occurred in Alaska. Within a very short time an urgent warning was sent to the Hawaiian Islands, some 5000 miles away, that the quake had generated a large seismic wave. At a specified hour the wave could strike the beaches of the islands.

The alarm system was put into action. Residents of the beach areas were warned to move to higher ground. Sirens were sounded; police officers even went from door to door with the message, making sure that no one would be left stranded.

All around the islands, sensible, reasonable people prepared to evacuate. But there were some who scoffed at the warnings. Others felt that they were far enough inland. A few even laughed at their neighbors, ''Oh, there's no real danger here. We've had warnings before and nothing happened. Relax. Don't worry about it. We're safe enough here.'' Not until they heard the dreadful wave thundering toward them did they believe. But by then it was too late.

Bar-Jesus not only refused to believe the message of salvation, but he also tried his best to keep Sergius Paulus from believing it as well. It is a terrible thing to hinder someone from hearing the story of Christ. The story of Jesus and His love is so important that we should never fail to treat it with true respect, for it is Jesus who is our Saviour and our Lord.

Xpand

Memorize

Today's Verse
"I am not ashamed of the gospel, because it is the power of God for the salvation of everyone who believes: first for the Jew, then for the Gentile.''

Romans 1:16

Primaries: Discuss with the students the meaning of the words *ashamed* and *gospel*. The rest of the words in the verse are probably part of the children's vocabulary, so you may use the chalkboard method to learn this verse. Print the verse on the chalkboard; ask the entire group to read it together. Repeat the verse until the group sounds confident. Then ask them to close their eyes and visualize the verse while you erase one of the words; ask the group to read the verse, supplying the missing word. Repeat the process until all the words are removed and only the Bible reference remains. Ask each student to recite the verse from memory.

Middlers/Juniors: Put the following phrases on separate cards: I am not ashamed / of the gospel, / because it is / the power of God / for the salvation of everyone who believes: / first for the Jew, / then for the Gentile. / Romans 1:16

Make enough sets of cards that children may work in groups of four students. Give each group a set of cards; tell the groups to put the cards in order so that the verse reads correctly. When a group has put its verse together, invite the individuals to take turns putting the cards in order after the others have mixed them up.

Memory Project
Psalm 1

This new project is a good reminder of the importance of God's word. For the people in Cyprus to be saved, they had to hear the word preached. Knowing God's word makes a difference in his life, as the psalmist describes.

Verse one could be learned with the question method used in lesson four. Verses three and four illustrate well.

Apply

This is a good opportunity for the children to think about what Jesus means to them and express what they think and feel.

Allow them time to think about the assignment you select; quiet music played while they think will make them more comfortable. Possible questions or assignments include: What does the gospel (good news about Jesus) mean to you? How does loving Jesus and God make your life different? What did you believe and feel when you accepted Jesus as your Savior? What word describes how you feel about Jesus? What is your favorite incident from Jesus' life? What fact about Jesus do you like best?

If you do this sharing in the large group, ask for volunteers to speak. If you break up into smaller groups, use circle response. In circle response no child may speak a second time until everyone has had a chance to speak once. It is good to let a child be allowed to repeat what someone else has said if that was also his/her thought. Don't let this activity be the source of embarrassment to any child.

Lesson Six
Acts 13:13-52

Xamine

Acts 13:13. Perga was the capital city. John Mark ended this journey with Paul and returned home to Jerusalem. Just why he left is not known, but whatever it was, his action at this time caused Paul to refuse to have him as a companion at a later time. Eventually he did prove his worth to Paul (Colossians 4:10).

13:14, 15. This Antioch is to be distinguished from the Antioch in Syria from which the journey had begun. On the Sabbath the travellers entered into the synagogue, continuing Paul's practice of going first to the Jews in each city. As was the custom, Jewish visitors to the synagogue were often asked if they had any message they would like to bring. This gave Paul his opportunity.

13:16. Paul wants to capture the attention of his hearers. *Ye that fear God* probably refers to persons in the audience who are converts to the Jewish faith, as yet uncircumcised.

13:17-22. Using his opportunity wisely, Paul first shows that he is a firm believer in the Old Testament Scriptures and the promises contained in them. As he recounts briefly the history of God's people, he reminds them of the promised Messiah.

13:23-33. Here Paul gives a very brief account of the life and death of Jesus, the Saviour of Israel. He begins by reminding them of John the Baptist whom many Jews had accepted and heeded.

13:34-41. Paul proceeds to show how Christ fulfilled the prophecies which the Jews cherished, quoting from Isaiah (vs. 34), David (Psalm 16:10), and Habakkuk (vs. 41).

13:42-44. Both Jews and Gentiles were eager to hear more of this message, and when Paul and Barnabas came as requested on the next Sabbath, a great multitude had gathered to hear them speak.

13:45. The word envy here speaks of wrath and indignation, for now the Jews begin to argue and contradict.

13:46-49. Because the Jews were rejecting the gospel, Paul states publicly that he is turning to the Gentiles. Amid great rejoicing, those Gentiles who were open to God's leading accepted Christ and the Word spread over the region.

13:50-52. The Jews carried their anger to those in places of high rank so that persecution began. Paul and Barnabas, leaving the new Christians rejoicing even in the midst of difficulties, went on to Iconium.

Xcite

As the children arrive, form pairs to be partners for the game, *Who's Your Partner?* This is an opportunity to help children pair up with someone other than a best friend.

Form two circles, one within the other, with the partners facing each other. Students in the inside circle turn to face a clockwise direction; the outside circle faces a counterclockwise direction. While music is played, the two circles march in the direction they are headed. When the music stops, those in the outside circle stand still until their partners return. Each player in the inside circle runs to his partner, joins hands with him, and they stoop. All stand up and the music starts again, with the two circles marching in opposite directions.

You have just played a game in which you learned to work well with your partner. In our Bible study today, one person in Paul's traveling group will drop out.

Teach two songs. The first one, "Come, Follow Jesus Wherever He Leads Us," 96, uses the familiar tune, "Chopsticks." It will be learned easily. Teach also, the song, "Offering Song," 99, to use before or during the offering.

Xpress

Order of Worship

Prelude
"We Gather Together," 105
Call to Worship: Psalm 95:1-3
"Happiness," 83
"We Will Go to All the World," 110
"Jesus Died for Men," 90
Communion
"Offering Song," 99
Offering
Introduction/Bible Story
Application Story
"Come, Follow Jesus," 96

Introduction

Display several light sources as objects for discussion (flashlight, lightbulb, match, candle, lamp).

Talk about these objects, how they give light, when and how each might be used and needed.

Light is valuable to each one of us. Without it we would die. Jesus spoke of Himself as being the Light of the World. We are told to be lights, reflecting God's love. Paul, when the Jews rejected his message, said that he had been appointed to be a light for the Gentiles. How thankful we can be that the Light of Life is for all mankind, for whosoever will take it and use it.

Bible Story

On the wall or overhead map trace Paul's journey thus far from Antioch. Show them where John Mark turned back and the rest of Paul's company continued, probably on foot, into this new land.

This story deals with people, showing how both the Jews and the Gentiles at first seemed eager to hear of Christ. Point out how carefully Paul handled the message in his attempt not to turn the Jews away, yet their pride and anger caused them to turn their backs on their Saviour. Paul was probably happy to see the acceptance of Jesus by the Gentiles, but he longed to bring his own people to a saving belief in Christ as Lord. It must have been with a great deal of sadness that he "shook off the dust" of that city.

Application Story

Mary was frightened. The night was very dark and she had to walk quite a distance down a long, lonely road, unlighted except for the cold stars high over her head. She had not meant to be this late but the hours had passed too quickly at Sally's house and early darkness had been on its way before she had started on her way home.

Mary didn't like the dark! Every bush looked like a huddled beast; tree branches made horrid, scraping noises. In the distance she could hear the howling of a dog. Her heart was pounding and pounding and her throat felt dry and tight.

Then, suddenly, she saw a lantern swinging along down the road toward her, coming around the curve that meant that she was half-way home. The cheerful voice of her brother called, "Come on, Mary; Mom sent me to meet you. She thought you would be glad of a light."

Paul had been sent with the light of salvation. The Jews should have been the ones who were most anxious of all to see that wonderful light from God, but they rejected it. They went on their way, stumbling in the dark.

Let's not reject the light that God has shown into our lives. Accepting Jesus, the Light of the World, makes our whole life have meaning and purpose. We want to joyously live in His light.

Xpand

Memorize

Today's Verse
"When Jesus spoke again to the people, he said, 'I am the light of the world. Whoever follows me will never walk in darkness, but will have the light of life.''

John 8:12

Use the series of pictures below on flash cards or a poster to illustrate the verse.

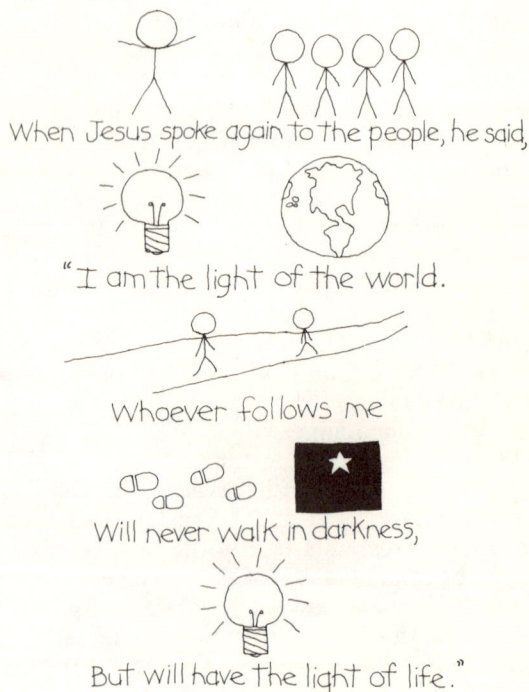

Apply

Photocopy enough copies of the game on page 69 so that you have a game for every two or three students. Bring buttons for playing pieces. As they play, students will follow the route of this first missionary journey. Encourage review conversations.

Directions
1. Cut out the numbered pieces and turn upside down in a pile.
2. Select a button and place it in Antioch.
3. Take turns drawing a numbered piece from the pile to know how many squares to move.
4. If you land on an opponent's square, he must return to Antioch unless his square is "safe."
5. You must draw the exact number to reach home.

Middlers/Juniors: As students complete their games, distribute their maps. Provide colored pencils from which they may select a new color for drawing the route of this first missionary journey. They may use their game boards as guides.

Lesson Seven
Acts 14:1-28

Xamine

Acts 14:1. Again in Iconium Paul and Barnabas speak in such a way that they are able to bring both Jews and Greeks to believe the message.

14:2. As is to be the pattern, the unbelieving Jews stir up trouble for the Christians.

14:3-7. Staying in this city for some time, Paul and Barnabas are given much power from the Holy Spirit to do signs and wonders. The work flourishes, but with continuing opposition from the Jews, the city divides into factions, for and against Paul. When violence erupts, Paul and his company flee the city, going on to Lystra and Derbe.

14:8-10. The man healed is a known cripple, never having walked from birth, so this miracle of healing causes great excitement.

14:11-13. Knowing that this miracle has divine origin, the people of Lystra naturally attribute it to the gods they know. It may be that Barnabas was a large man (thus, Jupiter) while Paul, the speaker, is called Mercury (the god of eloquence).

14:14-18. Paul and Barnabas were greatly troubled that the men of Lystra were calling them gods and tried to tell them about the true and living God. Tearing the clothing was a customary sign of intense grief and shock.

14:19, 20. The visiting Jews evidently had no trouble in swaying the fickle Lystrians. The group of sorrowing disciples almost certainly included Timothy (Acts 16:1). Some sort of miracle is involved in his recovery.

14:21-25. From Derbe they retrace their journey, encouraging these new congregations along the way. They also aided in the selection of elders or leaders in every church.

14:26-28. Having completed this first missionary tour, they return to Antioch of Syria and report on the wonderful ways in which God has blessed the work they had done.

Xcite

Play *The Lost Child* (see lesson one) to encourage your students again to become more aware of one another.

Teach the song, "We Worship God," page 104. Guide the children in understanding how it expresses their thoughts and praise to God.

Xpress

Order of Worship

Prelude
"We Worship God," 104
Call to Worship: Psalm 96:1-3
"We Praise Thy Name," 83
Prayer
"Happiness," 83
"Jesus Loves Me"
Communion
"Offering Song," 99
Offering
Introduction/Bible Story
Application Story
"We Will Go to All the World," 110

Introduction

Take a pocket mirror to class. Demonstrate the way in which it can shine a reflected light very brilliantly by flashing it around the room.

Wouldn't it be nonsense to insist that this mirror is a bright light? It is only a reflected light. In a dark room it would not be any kind of light at all, would it?

Paul and Barnabas were able to reflect the light of Christ as they journeyed for Him. The power they used was God's power and they gave Him the honor and the glory.

Demonstrate again how the power to flash leaves the mirror when the mirror is removed from the source of the light.

Our lives can show the light of Christ only when we allow Him to shine forth through us.

Bible Story

If you are tracing the journey on the map, travel with Paul first to Iconium, then on to Lystra. Tell the story of the exciting events in Lystra before going on to complete the rest of this journey—all the way back to Antioch in Syria. This is a favorite story, for there is a great deal of action contained in verses seven through twenty. The bravery of these servants of God as they face a confused and idolatrous people is truly inspiring.

Application Story

Johnny hadn't actually intended to cheat. Now he felt quite miserable about the way that things had worked out.

The teacher had assigned each pupil the task of writing a theme. Now Johnny hated to write anything, and especially something as hard as a theme. He was a bit lazy and writing took a lot of time and effort. As he sat flipping through an old notebook he had found he came across a theme that his mother had written when she must have been just about his age. Without giving his conscience much time to trouble him, he copied the theme very carefully and the next day he handed it in as though it were his own work.

Now he was in trouble. The teacher had liked the theme so well that she had asked him to read it aloud at the next assembly—and his parents were invited to attend!

Johnny was finding out the hard way that it doesn't pay to pretend to be something that you are not. He was faced with confessing either to his parents or his teacher. Whichever he chose, he would undoubtedly be in trouble with both.

Paul and Barnabas were wise enough to see that they must not accept honor for the miracle of healing. The power was God's power, not theirs. To have received the honor of the day would have been terribly wrong. Even though it meant difficulty for them they cried out, "We are men, like yourselves! Give God the honor and the praise!"

Apply

Plan a drama for the events of Acts 14:8-18. Write a narration for Primaries to pantomime. Middlers and Juniors will enjoy speaking simple lines from a script.

Actors needed are: crippled man, Paul, Barnabas, the crowd, and people of the crowd who speak out.

Carry out the drama twice. Between the two portrayals discuss why the people acted the way they did and why Paul and Barnabas answered as they did. Encourage the students to feel the roles and use expression as they act the second time.

Xpand

Memorize

Today's Verse

"Jesus answered, 'It is written: **"Worship the Lord your God and serve him only."** ' "

Luke 4:8

Explain the background of this verse taken from Jesus' temptations in the wilderness.

Antiphonal recitation will help the students learn this verse.

First group: "Jesus answered,
Second group: 'It is written:
First group: "Worship the Lord your God
Second group: and serve him only." ' "
Everyone: Luke 4:8

Memory Project
Psalm 1

Lesson Eight
Acts 15:36-41; 16:1-3

Xamine

Acts 15:36. The interval between the first and second journey is not certain. It included a "long time" (Acts 14:28), a visit to Jerusalem (15:1-29) and "some days" as mentioned in this verse.

Now Paul suggests to Barnabas that they go and revisit the young churches which they had helped to establish on their first journey.

15:37. John Mark was Barnabas' nephew and it is not surprising that he wants to give the young man a second chance.

15:38. Whatever John Mark's reason for not completing the first journey, Paul now feels that he should not be permitted to travel with them again.

15:39. This verse shows clearly that differences can and do occur between brothers, enough so that they cannot work together. There is no evidence that either of them ever said an unkind word about the other afterward. Also, Paul later has praise for John Mark saying that he is "profitable to me for the ministry" (2 Timothy 4:11).

15:40. Now, however, Barnabas having taken John Mark and gone to Cyprus, Paul chooses Silas who had come up from Jerusalem, and they begin their journey in the opposite direction.

15:41. This confirmation refers to strengthening the churches.

16:1. In the church at Lystra Paul finds the young man Timothy, the son of a Jewish-Christian mother, Eunice, and a Grecian father. Timothy's grandmother was also a Christian (2 Timothy 1:5). Timothy was evidently a young man.

16:2. Timothy had a good reputation both in his home church and in the church in the adjoining town.

16:3. Since Timothy's father was a Greek, Timothy had not been circumcised. Paul had him undergo this Jewish ritual in order to keep from raising unnecessary controversy among Jews.

Xcite

Since your students are studying how the gospel was taken to other countries from Jerusalem, it should be interesting to them to play a game from another country, Japan. (If your church supports a missionary in Japan, use this opportunity to describe briefly the work.)

In this Japanese game, children form a circle with one player in the middle. The player in the middle taps his nose three times and then his mouth as he says, "Hana, hana, hana, kuchi" (nose, nose, nose, mouth). The children forming the circle follow his lead, touching their noses and mouths as he does. The second time he repeats the phrase, the center player may touch any features in any order, regardless of the words he is saying. The other children try to follow his actions rather than his words.

Teach the song, "If God Be For Us," page 98. Emphasize the importance of the words of the song; discuss with the children some of the "tough" times that God will be with them.

Xpress

Order of Worship

"We Worship God," 104
Call to Worship: Psalm 105:1-3 or Psalm 1
"If God Be For Us," 98
"Come, Follow Jesus," 96
"Happiness," 83
"Jesus Died for Men," 90
Communion
Offering
"We Will Go to All the World"
Introduction/Bible Story
Application Story

Introduction

Music exercise books will be helpful in illustrating the lesson for today. If possible, have a very simple book, a slightly harder one, and one with quite difficult pieces. It would be effective if you could have someone play a brief portion from each book, showing the work that is necessary to move from one level of ability to another.

All of us can start to learn to do something. Maybe it is not music that you want to learn. No matter what it is that you set out to learn, if you are ever going to be really good at it, if you are going to make real progress, you are going to have to have the strength of mind and body to stick with it.

John Mark, on that first journey, simply was not willing to stick to the work that needed to be done.

Paul had no confidence in him at this time that he would not again prove to be unreliable. How sad this was for John Mark, for Barnabas, and for Paul.

Bible Story

This lesson need not be negative. Even though John Mark failed to complete his mission and for a time became the source of conflict between Paul and Barnabas, the work of God went right on and grew. It is good to point out that even when we make mistakes (like John Mark), or have problems among us (like Paul and Barnabas) God can still use us if we will let Him. Paul and Barnabas still loved each other. Have the class find the gospel of Mark in their Bibles. Ask them who wrote this wonderful story of the life of Jesus. It was John Mark. He went on from this point in his life to become a wonderful worker for the Lord.

Application Story

James was eager to be on the basketball team. He was delighted when the coach noticed that he was able to shoot baskets with ease. James knew that not only was he fast and a good shot, but he was also tall—and that's a real help when it comes to basketball. When the coach selected him, he was greatly excited.

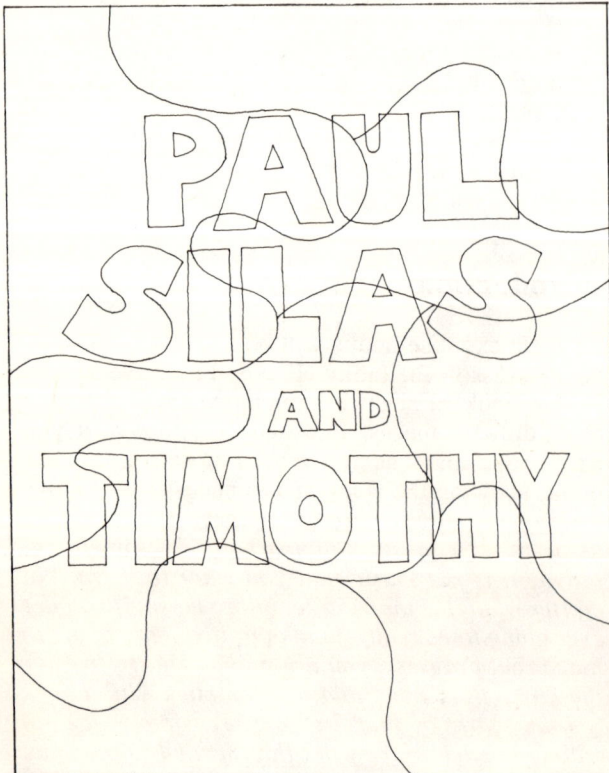

"I'm really on the team, ready to play on the first string," he thought with delight.

But basketball takes lots of practice, lots of real work. To be really good you have to give up some other activities. James found out that this was not all fun. It was hard! He began to miss a practice now and then. Eventually he just dropped out. He didn't have what it took to stick it out through the long hours of practice and discipline.

His place was taken by Andrew, for there were others waiting and eager to be on the team. Andrew was not as tall and his basket work was not as sure and certain as James' had been, but Andrew was willing to work hard.

John Mark, too, was not willing to keep going when the journey became difficult. He quit. Although he later became a great worker for the Lord, he missed out on the wonderful experience of working and travelling with Paul.

Xpand

Memorize

Today's Verse
"Whatever you do, work at it with all your heart, as working for the Lord, not for men."

Colossians 3:23

Singing this verse to the tune of "Here We Go 'Round the Mulberry Bush," will help your students learn the words. Sing it in this way:
Whatever you do, whatever you do,
   Work at it, work at it,
With all your heart, as working for the Lord,
   Not for men.

Memory Project
Psalm 1
Have any of your students recited this psalm yet for worship?

Apply

Primaries: Photocopy the puzzle on page 70 for the students. Provide crayons and scissors. Allow the students to color the puzzle and then cut apart to make a puzzle. As they reassemble the puzzle, review facts about the travelers.

Middlers/Juniors: With the students brainstorm some situations when boys and girls might disagree with one another in a Bible-school class, children's church session, or youth group meeting. Be ready with some ideas from your observations. Select a few examples to act out and discuss how to behave with love.

Lesson Nine

Acts 16:4-15

Xamine

Acts 16:4. As Paul, Silas, and Timothy travelled through the cities in which there were congregations, one of the things that they did was to deliver to the Christians the decisions made by the council in Jerusalem concerning the Jewish law as it applied to the Christian faith (see Acts 15:20-22).

16:5. The acceptance of these Gentile Christians by the respected brethren in Jerusalem had a very positive effect on the churches.

16:6, 7. Paul and his company travelled through Phrygia and Galatia but when they wanted to go first into Asia (probably Asia Minor) and then to Bithynia, the Spirit did not permit them to do so.

16:8, 9. Still not sure where God wanted them to go next, but certain where he did *not* want them to go, they proceeded on down to Troas. The vision gives them their next destination.

16:10. Note that the pronoun *we* is used here, indicating that Luke, the author of the book of Acts, is now journeying with them. It may be that he joined them at about this point.

16:11. Wasting no time, they take a ship from Troas. to Macedonia

16:12. The vision had not been specific as to just where in Macedonia they should go, so they went to Philippi, an important city of the area as well as being a Roman colony. There they waited for God's direction.

16:13. After waiting there for a few days they went, as was their continuing custom, to meet with a group of Jews who met for prayer by a riverside.

16:14. The group gathered at this river were evidently all or largely women. Among them was an important businesswoman, Lydia, who made her living by selling purple dye or purple cloth used by the wealthy. Lydia received the words spoken by Paul with an open heart.

16:15. Not only Lydia, but others in her household came to believe and were baptized. Then she urged Paul and his company to come and stay in her home. Not only was she showing great hospitality but she would, through their visit to her home, have further opportunity to learn.

Xcite

For a review of the first eight lessons play *Read and Do*. Place a jar or box on a table. Let volunteers go one at a time to the box and pick out a slip of paper. He reads it to the rest of the children and then does what it says. Help the children who are learning to read.

Some possibilities to write on the slips of paper are: say a Bible verse, lead the class in singing a song, tell what was laid at Saul's feet when Stephen was stoned, tell about a time when it took a lot of courage for you to do something, describe the way Saul left Damascus, list at least two things you like about Barnabas, locate on the map a city where Paul preached.

Teach the song, "We Look to Jesus," page 100. Ask the children what people in these lessons about Paul might have been willing to sing that song. Examples, Stephen was willing to "even die for Him" and the Christians who taught about Jesus when they moved away from the persecution in Jerusalem could sing "let's be faithful."

Xpress

Order of Worship

Prelude
Call to Worship: Psalm 107:1, 2, 9 or Psalm 1
"We Praise Thy Name," 83
"If God Be for Us," 98
"We Look to Jesus," 100
"Jesus Loves Me"
Communion
"Offering Song," 99
Offering
Introduction/Bible Story
Application Story
Prayer

Introduction

Display some travel brochures, maps, and pictures of interesting places to visit.

Most of us like to travel. Look at these pictures. Wouldn't you like to have the chance to visit some of these places? Allow discussion. *Sometimes we travel by choice (vacation) and sometimes because it is necessary (a move or business trip). Sometimes we like where we go; sometimes we are disappointed.*

As we go here and there through our lives, there is one thing that it is good for us to remember. God can use us wherever we may go. Whether we stay right close to home or travel around the world, we can still work for Jesus.

Bible Story

Trace Paul's journey on the map as you go through this lesson. It is probable that the company of missionaries was travelling on foot from one city to another. During this first part of the second journey, the aim was to meet with and strengthen the young congregations along the way, sharing with them the encouraging message of acceptance sent by the leaders of the church in Jerusalem.

Help the class to realize how frustrating it must have been to find that the Lord did not want them to go into the areas where they had thought that they should go. Yet they were obedient to His direction and waited for Him to show them the way.

In Philippi they still did not know to whom the Lord was sending them. It was their openness and their willingness to find the Lord's leading that brought them to Lydia and the group of faithful women who were meeting on the Sabbath to worship God. God was opening the door for the gospel and though this may have seemed to be a very humble beginning, the cause of Christ would prosper because they were willing to hear and obey.

Application Story

Have you ever wanted to do something so badly that you felt that you just had to get your own way? Probably everyone has had this experience. It is hard to be calm and patient when we can't get something that we want very, very much.

Janet wanted to go to camp. She prayed that she would get to go. She saved up her own money for the camp fees and worked at extra jobs to get some extra spending money. Since her mother was not sure that Janet was old enough to go off alone,

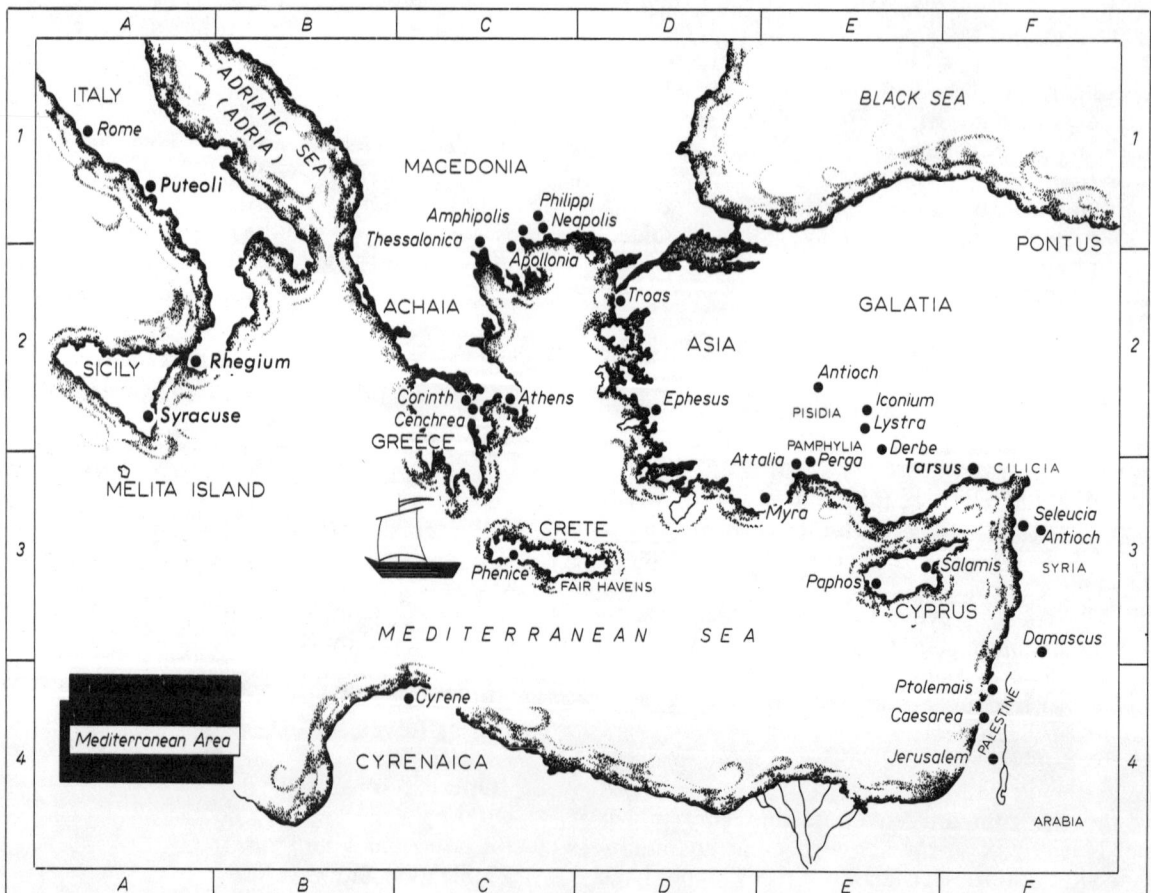

Mediterranean Area

28

Janet helped clean the house and did all of her regular chores without complaining so that her mother would see just how reliable she had become.

One week before camp, her mother gave final approval. Janet was all set to leave on Monday morning. Then, on Sunday evening Janet slipped on the porch step and broke her leg! All her planning and preparation had been for nothing!

As Janet spent the long hours in her hospital bed, thinking about all the fun that her friends were having, she felt dreadfully sad and angry. Why had this happened to her? Hadn't she prayed? She had tried so hard to be good and do what was right! Why? Why? Why?

In the bed next to her lay a thin, pale little girl. At first Janet did not want to notice her. She wanted to think about her own problems and disappointments. Yet gradually she became more and more aware of the listless sadness in her companion. As one day followed another, Janet began to try to talk to Sue. Lying there side by side, Janet's naturally loving and caring self reached out and little by little she got Sue to talk to her. Before many days passed, the girls became friends.

One day the doctor, on his rounds, heard the two girls chattering happily. He gave a delighted smile as he turned to the nurse. "Miss Barton, it is wonderful that Janet Gray came to the hospital. I was seriously concerned about Sue. She was drifting away from us no matter what medicine we gave her. Now she is eating better and her eyes look bright with the love of life. Janet's broken leg was a real blessing to us—and to Sue."

Paul must have been bitterly disappointed when he was not permitted to go to Asia. Yet he knew that God had a greater purpose for him in Macedonia. Wherever we are, and whatever our disappointments or frustrations, God can use us to His glory—if we let Him.

Xpand

Memorize

Today's Verse
"Show me your ways, O Lord,
   Teach me your paths;
guide me in your truth and teach me,
   for you are God my Savior,
     and my hope is in you all day long."
                    Psalm 25:4, 5

Primaries: Use flash cards with the key words from the verse.
   Show me your *ways*, O *Lord*,
   teach me your *paths*.
   Psalm 25:4

Middlers/Juniors: Give each student six large index cards (4 x 6 or 5 x 7). Write the Bible verses on the chalkboard. Underline the key words.
   Show me your *ways*, O *Lord*,
   teach me your *paths*;
   guide me in your *truth* and *teach* me,
   for you are *God my Savior*,
   and my *hope* is in you *all day* long.
                 Psalm 25:4, 5

Read the verses with the students two or three times. Discuss how it relates to today's lesson. Draw attention to the words underlined. Suggest that they are key words that might help them memorize the verses if they write them on their own cards. One line goes on each card. Thus, the students' first card would read Show me your ways, O Lord. If a student wants to write more words on his card, be flexible.

Memory Project
New Testament Books
If your students can't recite the names of the books of the New Testament, assign this as an extra project. As they work, or recite, talk with them about which books were written by Paul. Help them associate the name of the book with the people and the city. For example, today they began studying about the Christians in Philippi to whom he wrote Philippians.

Apply

Primaries: These new readers will enjoy finding the message about Lydia by writing down every second letter from the circle in the puzzle on page 71. The puzzle answer is "a place of prayer is where Lydia was."

Middlers/Juniors: Begin work on the route of Paul's second journey. Distribute the students' maps and colored pencils. Instruct the students to find Antioch. Guide them in drawing a route beginning there and traveling through Syria and Cilicia to Derbe, Lystra, Iconium, and Antioch through Asia to Troas to Neapolis to Philippi.

As you mention each city and province ask the children what they remember about the events in each city.

Lesson Ten
Acts 16:16-22

Xamine

Acts 16:16. On their way to the place of prayer (perhaps down by the river) the company is met by a young woman, a slave, who earned money for her owners by telling fortunes.

16:17. Just what prompted this unfortunate girl to follow Paul is not stated, but follow she did and loudly proclaimed that they were from God.

16:18. This continued for several days. Paul did not want to be proclaimed by an evil spirit. No doubt he also felt compassion for this girl and he reprimanded, not the girl, but the spirit which had taken over her being.

16:19. The marketplace to which the girl's owners took Paul and Silas was undoubtedly where the courts would be meeting to hear grievances.

16:20. Laying charges that would be the most damaging, the owners accused Paul and Silas of troubling the city—emphasizing that they were Jews.

16:21. Obviously these men did not really care about the customs and laws of Rome. They simply wanted to get Paul and Silas into as much trouble as they could.

16:22. It was not hard to turn the crowd against these Jewish strangers. The rulers, willing to go along with the wishes of the multitude, commanded a public beating.

Xcite

Because of your attitude and emphasis during these weeks, your students should know one another's names and be more alert to observing who is present. Today's game, *Who Is It?*, will help more.

One pupil leaves the room. On returning, he is told that the others have selected one of the children in the room and that he must guess who it is. He tries to find out by asking one question at a time of each child in the circle. Each question must be answerable by "yes," "no," or "I don't know." If the player asks only surface questions like the color of clothing, encourage him/her to ask questions about hobbies, interests, and family.

Teach the song, "My God Is a Great God," page 91. Ask how knowing that God is a great God would help someone to do what he/she knows is right. Discuss how comforting and strengthening it is to know that God is with you even if no one else is.

Xpress

Order of Worship

Prelude
"We Gather Together," 97
Call to Worship: Isaiah 55:6
"My God Is a Great God," 91
"Jesus Died for Men," 90
Communion
Offering
Introduction/Bible Story
Application Story
"If God Be for Us," 98

Introduction

Here is a very brief true or false quiz. Decide in your mind whether the sentence is true or false.

1. It is wrong to tattle on someone. True or false?

2. It is right to keep a secret. True or false?

3. It is wrong to do what others tell you to do. True or false?

4. It is right to listen to others. True or false?

It is pretty obvious that when we try to give these statements a definite true or false decision, we run into all kinds of questions. There may come times when we have to decide to do something that will make others angry with us, but if we know that it is the wise and right thing to do, we should follow our consciences.

In today's story we will see that Paul did something that made some men very angry. His action caused them to lose a lot of money. Yet Paul felt that his action was right and just, and he was brave enough to do it even though it brought on a lot of difficulty.

Bible Story

Remind students that Paul had not intended to go to Macedonia. Paul obeyed God's instruction and went there even though he could not understand why he could not go to Asia.

In Philippi they met Lydia. When she and her family accepted Christ, Paul must have thought, "Lord, now I see why you wanted me to come here."

Now, in today's story, Paul begins on a whole new adventure, though not a pleasant one at all. Yet Paul knows that God is showing that He has further use for him in this city. God knows what is ahead for us and He can use us if we let Him.

Application Story

Tim walked along the road, scuffling his feet in the dust. A scowl darkened his usually cheerful face. It would be bad enough to be in trouble if he had done something wrong—but he'd been trying to do right—trying to be good. Now he was in trouble anyhow.

The gang had decided that it would be fun to climb up and cross the long railroad bridge that spanned the river outside of town. Trains did not come often, and they thought it would be safe. They knew that there was some danger, but they wanted some exciting fun.

Maybe he should have just let them get in trouble—or hurt. At least then they wouldn't be mad at him. He could have just refused to join in the game and let them go on if they chose. But Tim knew that it was really dangerous! One slip and they would fall! Someone might even be killed and he did not want to take a chance on that happening. Now he could still hear their words ringing in his ears. "You Tattle-tale! Have to spoil our fun just because you're chicken."

Tim knew something of how Paul may have felt as he was punished there in Philippi. Paul had done something good, something right. He had saved a young slave girl and freed her from a terrible oppression. The thanks that he got was a beating.

It is hard to receive ill for our good behavior. Yet that is the way that it happens sometimes. We can be comforted, though, as Paul was, when we remember that Jesus, our Lord, suffered when He had done no wrong. We who love and follow Him can expect to receive some difficulties too.

Xpand

Memorize

Today's Verse
"Blessed are those who are persecuted
   because of righteousness,
for theirs is the kingdom of heaven."
                              Matthew 5:10

Explain the meaning of the new words, then ask how they would put the verse into their own words.

Display the verse written on a poster in thought segments like this:
                   Blessed are those
                who are persecuted
              because of righteousness,
                    for theirs is
              the kingdom of heaven.
                   Matthew 5:10

Read the verse together several times, letting the children concentrate on the thought segments. Read it antiphonally several times with half the students reading the first three lines and the other half reading the last two lines. Exchange reading assignments. Recite the verse several times without the poster in view.

Apply

Select fourteen volunteers to prepare the Bible drama on pages 73 and 74. Give each child a copy of the script. Enlist the people in the crowd to be your stage crew so that the two scenes can be set up quickly and quietly.

The drama is to be presented next Sunday between the introduction and Bible story. That allows Xcite time next week to be a final rehearsal. If you want the children to memorize their parts and the production to be elaborate, it will be necessary to hold a rehearsal during the week. Use a little time before/after such a rehearsal to serve refreshments and get to know the children better.

The rest of the students may play one of the following games using their memory verses. (If they are memorizing verses in Bible school, add them to the possibilities.)

Shout the Word: The children divide into two teams and sit in rows facing one another. The first teacher selects a Bible verse; each player of the team is given one word of the verse. On signal all the children shout their words in unison. When the other team has guessed the verse, the members recite it in unison.

Take Us If You Can: This is a variation of the game, "New Orleans." Children divide into two teams and sit in rows facing one another. The challenging team gives a Scripture reference and the other team must quote the Scripture. If that team fails, the challengers quote the verse and select a member of the other team for their team. (If only popular or smart children are being chosen, set up a system for selection.)

31

Lesson Eleven
Acts 16:23-40

Xamine

Acts 16:23. Jewish law dictated forty stripes but Roman law set no limit and in 2 Corinthians 11:23 Paul refers to having been given "stripes above measure." Severely beaten, they are thrown into prison.

16:24. The inner prison was the most secure part. Their feet were probably tied by cords to a beam of wood; they could neither sit nor stand without pain.

16:25. In great discomfort, Paul and Silas were not able to sleep. Instead of bewailing their fate, they spent those difficult hours in prayer and praise. No doubt the other prisoners were astounded by their behavior.

16:26. The earthquake certainly proclaimed God's presence among them.

16:27. According to the Roman code it was better to commit suicide than to suffer death at the executioner's hand which would happen if the prisoners escaped.

16:28, 29. The jailer called for lights to examine the prison.

16:30. It seems that the jailer had some previous knowledge of the mission of these two prisoners. Now the jailer turns to them for the answer to the most important question a person can ask.

16:31, 32. Beginning with the great need that each person has for faith in Jesus Christ, Paul goes on to tell the jailer and all in his house the word of the Lord.

16:33, 34. As soon as he knew what was required of him, the jailer humbly ministered to the wounds from the beatings and that same hour he and his family were baptized.

16:35, 36. The magistrates had had time to consider their actions and had decided that they should release these prisoners. The jailer must have been happy to give the message that Paul and Silas were to go free.

16:37, 38. Paul's refusal to slip quietly away was a great surprise and when the officials realized that they had beaten a Roman citizen without due trial, they were alarmed.

16:39. The magistrates were afraid because they had violated Roman law.

16:40. Before leaving Philippi, Paul and Silas return to Lydia's home. They take time to comfort (encourage) the Christians there before departing.

Xcite

As students arrive, send the drama group away for final rehearsal. Organize the others into two teams for *Play Another Note.*

The pianist (or guitarist) plays three or four notes from one of the songs the children have been singing in children's church. Any child on either team who thinks he knows the title raises his hand and the leader calls on the first one to volunteer. If that player guesses correctly, his team wins five points; otherwise the opposing team wins one point. After an incorrect guess, any player from the opposition may, if he wishes, guess the song to get the five points. If he too is incorrect, his team loses the one point. If neither team guesses correctly, the game leader adds a note to the three or four he already played. The game goes on as before—with more notes added after each round—until the song title has been named. Action continues in this manner until one team—the winner—amasses 21 points.

We have been playing a music game because singing is an important part of today's lesson. Let's learn a song that describes what happened to Paul and Silas after last week's lesson. Teach "Paul and Silas," page 88.

Xpress

Order of Worship

Prelude
"We Worship God," 104
Call to Worship: Psalm 150:1, 2
"If God Be for Us," 98
"Happiness," 83
"Jesus Loves Me"
Communion
"Offering Song," 99
Offering
Introduction
Drama
Bible Story
Application Story
"Paul and Silas," 88
Prayer

Introduction

A length of chain, rope, a padlock, etc. can provide an object lesson for today's study. Discuss these articles as things which can bind a person or hold him prisoner.

It would be very uncomfortable to be locked up or restricted with one or more of these things, wouldn't it? No one wants to be tied up dor long, or locked away from the rest of the world. It is a natural instinct to want to be free.

Yet it doesn't take a jail cell to make you a prisoner and you are not always free even when you can run around and work or play. A person needs to be free within himself. The person who is at peace with God and with himself will know that he is truly free. No matter how difficult the circumstances (even locked in jail like Paul and Silas), the person who is free from sin is able to praise God.

Bible Story

The last lesson ended on a note of suspense. Let's review it by listening and watching the play our drama group has prepared.

Immediately following the drama continue the account.

With an earthquake and an attempted suicide, this has all the elements to make an exciting, inspiring story. There is a great lesson in this story for everyone whether it is for a Christian who needs to learn to praise God even in times of trouble or for the person who needs to ask this vital question, "What must I do to be saved."

Application Story

The little bird sat on the floor of the cage, his wings drooping, his eyes dull. It was a terrible thing to be a captured bird, cooped up here for the rest of his life. He was meant to fly free and joyfully sing as he soared into the blue sky. He could not bear this life in a cage. He would soon die.

Suddenly he heard a burst of beautiful song. He raised his head and saw, to his amazement, a little canary singing as though his heart were bursting with joy.

"How can you sing? Aren't you a prisoner—doomed to sit forever behind these bars? Doesn't your heart yearn to fly out and away? I do not understand how you can sing so joyously!"

The canary paused in his lilting song. "Yes, my sad friend, I will never know the joys of freedom. But being in a cage doesn't mean that I cannot praise Him who made me and gave me a voice to sing. I have found happiness and contentment even as a prisoner because I can lift my heart in song."

Paul and Silas knew that they could still praise God. Bleeding and in pain, they were able to witness to those around them as they honored their Heavenly Father.

Xpand

Memorize

Today's Verse
"Sing to the Lord a new song;
  sing to the Lord, all the earth.
Sing to the Lord, praise his name;
  proclaim his salvation day after day."
Psalm 96:1, 2

These verses can be learned by fitting them to the tune, "Happy Birthday." Run "to the" together on each line; use the two notes on "name;" add a pattern of four notes at the end.

If you cannot get it to fit the tune, use an antiphonal recitation. Let one group (Primaries, if you have them) read the words "Sing to the Lord" and the other group complete the sentence; both groups read the last line together.

Memory Project
Is knowing the order of the books of the New Testament helping the students find Bible verses? Do they feel more confident searching for New Testament books? An old-fashioned Bible drill might demonstrate to them how much they are learning and how it helps them to locate Bible references.

Apply

The Bible drama preparation and presentation probably gives you less time today. If you do have any time left after memorizing, ask the actors to tell the group how they felt at various points in the play as the characters. For example, ask the girl how she felt when Paul and Silas sent the spirit out of her.

Sing songs that the students think they might sing if they were in jail because they had been doing what God would want them to do.

Lesson Twelve
Acts 17:1-15

Xamine

Acts 17:1, 2. Amphipolis and Apollonia are both cities of Macedonia; Thessalonica is a seaport, an important city of this second part of Macedonia. It is probable that there were no synagogues in the first two cities.

17:3. Using the Scriptures that the Jews respected and believed, Paul attempted to show that Jesus is the Christ.

17:4. Note the three types who believed; some of the Jews, many of the devout Greeks (ones who had already given up idol worship and were ready to learn), and a number of the important women of the area.

17:5. Such success caused great envy among the nonbelievers who used some wicked men (whom they probably hired) to stir up the city to violence. Jason is mentioned by Paul in Romans 16:21 and may have been a relative with whom Paul and Silas were staying.

17:7-9. With no real charge against Jason, they let him go free, having made him pay a fine or pledge.

17:11. The Bereans receive a great compliment from Luke, the author.

17:12. Being willing to study the Scriptures with an open heart, many of the people of Berea came to believe.

17:13. The anger of the people of Thessalonica had not cooled and they were able to stir up trouble in Berea as well.

17:14, 15. Since Paul is the one most resented, he alone is sent on ahead. Silas and Timothy could stay to give further teaching.

Xcite

Play *Helpers Pantomime* this morning to introduce the theme of helping that will be exemplified later this morning by Jason.

Place on a table or stand a bowl containing slips of paper on which you have written ways that children can help Jesus.

As children arrive, form pairs. Let each pair draw a slip of paper from the bowl; they then may go off by themselves to plan how to act out the idea. (You may have to help Primaries read their instructions.)

Seat the children in a semicircle. Let each pair act out its idea in front of the others, and ask the rest of the group to guess.

Teach the song, "Let the Word of Christ Dwell in You," page 84. A discussion of the words of the song should include a search of Colossians 3:16, 17 by older students to see which group of words is quoted from the Bible.

Xpress

Order of Worship

Prelude
Call to Worship: Psalm 24:1, 9, 10
"We Praise Thy Name," 83
"We Look to Jesus," 100
"Jesus Died for Men," 90
Communion
"Offering Song," 99
Offering
Introduction/Bible Story
Application Story
"Let the Words of Christ Dwell in You," 84
Prayer

Introduction

Bring a rope and a glass of water—both items which in themselves are pretty ordinary, yet they can be the means of saving a life.

Show the rope. *Just suppose that you're stranded on a cliff and someone throws you a rope so that you can climb to safety.*

Hold up your hand. *Or maybe you are in deep water and are afraid that you will drown. Someone reaches out with his hand, grasps you and lifts you back into shallow water or into a boat.*

Or just imagine that you are out on the desert. You are lost and have drunk the very last of your water. Your throat is dry and burning and you are in danger of dying in great misery when suddenly a stranger comes riding across the sand and he gives you a cool drink of water. Show glass of water.

Now you may never save anyone's life but there are many seemingly small, unimportant things that can prove to be a great help to someone else. God gives us many opportunities to be of help—let's use them.

Bible Story

There are many people in history who have helped others in time of need. Their names may never be remembered by historians, but they were very important. Every great man has had such helpers in his life, giving courage and help when it was needed. Today's story includes one of these almost unknown helpers.

In your account emphasize the fact that the Bereans searched the Scriptures to see if what Paul said was true. It is not too early to train your students to test all teaching by the Bible.

Application Story

"No one will even notice I'm here," thought Jim. "I might just as well have stayed home."

Jim had come with his parents to visit his grandparents. The problem was that lots of other people had come too. All his aunts and uncles and cousins had come. There were relatives he had never seen before; little babies, middle-sized babies, people near his age and big grown-up cousins. Jim was shy and he felt that the best thing for him to do was to find a quiet corner and get out of the way.

Once safe in his corner, Jim began to watch what was going on around him. Everyone was hurrying around, talking and laughing. The women were chattering away in the kitchen, getting into each other's way. The men were talking to each other about the world and money and the government. Jim saw the children heading out to play some game but he didn't know how to join them. He felt very much left out and out of place.

Then he noticed someone whom no one was paying much attention to. There was one little old lady sitting off to the side, quite alone. Because she was alone, Jim felt interested in her. Forgetting himself and his feelings for the moment, he moved very quietly nearer to her and smiled at her.

To his surprise and pleasure, she smiled back with a sweet, warm smile. Not sure what he should

say next, Jim said softly, "Hi, I'm Jim. Can I do anything for you?"

"Jim, I'm your great-aunt Sally and I was just sitting here wishing some one would get me a glass of lemonade. I'll tell you how to get us each one." *And before long she and Jim were sitting side by side, sipping from frosty glasses—and Jim had found a friend.*

Jim had not done anything very big or very important, but he had come along and been ready and willing to be a friend and a helper when help was needed.

Xpand

Memorize

Today's Verse
"Let the word of Christ dwell in you richly as you teach and admonish one another with all wisdom, and as you sing psalms, hymns and spiritual songs with gratitude in your hearts to God."

Colossians 3:16

The students already know the first clause of the verse from the song, and that will be the entire verse for the Primaries. Middlers and Juniors can learn the rest of the verse by noting the parallel structure (as/with) of the rest of the verse. *"As you* teach and admonish one another *with* wisdom, and *as you* sing psalms, hymns and spiritual songs *with* gratitude in your hearts to God."

Memory Project
Books of the New Testament
By now your students should be completing this project. Give whatever recognition has been promised.

Apply

Sing the song, "B-I-B-L-E," again. Remind the students of the importance of knowing God's Word and then give them instructions for a Bible verse sharing time.

Use this procedure: seat the students in a circle or a circle within a circle; everyone sing "B-I-B-L-E"; one student recites a Bible verse; everyone sings "B-I-B-L-E"; one student recites a Bible verse; etc. If your group is large, you can divide into smaller groups, or let two or three students recite between the singing of the song.

If you have not been doing the memory work, let the children read a Bible verse of their choice.

Lesson Thirteen
Acts 17:16-34

Xamine

Acts 17:16. Paul was greatly disturbed by this city that was full of idols. Petronius wrote that it was easier to find a god than a man in Athens.

17:17. This time emphasis is given to his work between Sabbaths.

17:18. Epicureans did not believe in either a God of creation or gods interested in human affairs. Epicurus had felt that pleasure is the chief good and the followers had degraded his ideas to the place where they sought the sensual satisfaction of their appetites. Stoics believed in a God of creation who, like his creation, was ruled by immovable fate or Fates. They were very stern and rigid in their lifestyle. Now Paul has attracted the attention of these philosophers because his teachings are strange and disturbing.

17:19, 20. The philosophers were interested enough to lead Paul away to a quieter place. It was the meeting place of the court of Athens, but there is no indication that court was in session.

17:21. This parenthetical statement is a clear description of the general character of the philosophers and students of Athens. They enjoyed speculation and questioning; anything new was of great fascination.

17:22. Superstitious should read "very religious."

17:23. Paul seized upon the altar to an unknown god as a good introduction for his message.

17:24-27. This is a beautiful description of our God. He is deeply concerned and involved in us as His creation—giving us life and setting us on this beautiful earth that we may have the opportunity to seek and know Him—for He is not far from any of us.

17:28. This verse demonstrates Paul's desire to reach the hearts and minds of these questioning people as he turns to Greek phrases and quotations with which they are familiar.

17:29-31. Having established that man is God's special creation, Paul proceeds to try to show them how God intended mankind to honor Him. He tells them of the need of repentance and of Jesus whose resurrection proved the validity of His mission.

17:32. None of these Greeks believed in the resurrection from the dead. Many would hear him no further. Others, probably of the Stoics, determined to hear him again.

17:33, 34. When Paul left Mars Hill some of his hearers had begun to believe and later firmly embraced these teachings of Christ. Among them was a member of the council.

Xcite

For a review of the lessons thus far, play *Question, Anyone?* Cut a large question mark out of colored poster board. Punch holes large enough to hold folded-up pieces of paper containing questions.

One of the leaders may write out the questions, or you may allow each student to write out a question on a piece of paper. These questions will get you started: What did Saul do at Stephen's stoning? Where were the believers first called Christians? What could the slave girl in Philippi do that earned money for her owners?

Divide the group into teams. Let the players take turns selecting a question from the question mark.

Teach the song, "Stand Up, Sing Out," page 93. In your discussion of the song, ask the children about the feelings the words and music express.

Xpress

Order of Worship

Prelude
"We Worship God," 104
Call to Worship: Psalm 117
"If God Be for Us," 98
Prayer
"Jesus Loves Me"
Communion
"Offering Song," 99
Offering
Introduction/Bible Story
"Stand Up, Sing Out," 93
Prayer

Introduction

Obtain a toy car, a dollar, and a ball for this lesson.

We don't worship idols, do we? Of course not! But have you ever thought about the fact that we can make idols out of things? (Show objects one by one)

Some people seem to worship their cars. Each week they wash and polish it. They work on it and save up to buy more things for the car.

Some people make money their god. It rules their lives, their time, their interest.

Others seem to worship fun, giving almost all their time and attention to games, sports, and movies.

Now there is nothing wrong with enjoying your car, nor in earning money, nor in being a sports fan. These things are not wrong in themselves. Yet anything that becomes so important to us that it takes up too much of our lives can become an idol to us. Of course we don't kneel and pray to it, but it can hold our love and attention and keep us away from the Lord. Let's be careful to keep God in first place in our lives.

Bible Story

Take the class to Athens with you today. Go with them through this great and beautiful city. Help them to see the sadness of a people devoted to religion but who did not know God.

Those people of Athens who were fascinated by that which is new are not unlike people today. In our 20th century we are constantly faced with new ideas, inventions, situations. We, too, need to stop our frantic searching and look to God and His Son Jesus who are never "far from every one of us."

Application Story

A timid kimono-clad figure climbed the many steps to the ancient temple. In her hands she clutched a small Japanese doll. At the door she bowed low again and again before the huge statue of Buddha that seemed to guard the entry. This statue was not beautiful. It was fat and ugly and draped with stone-carved snakes. Yet this little lady bowed in deep reverence, for this was her god.

Inside the temple she went to a special section where she could offer up a special prayer. With eager pride she slipped the little doll into a small cubicle and she bowed again. She wanted a child and she was using this means to pray for a baby.

She did not know of our God who made heaven and earth, in whom we move and have our being.

Like the people in Athens, she was very religious, but her worship was in ignorance.

Paul was grieved to see those who wanted to worship but who did not know the true and living God, our Heavenly Father.

Since we are greatly blessed in knowing God and having Jesus as our Savior, let's give thanks and show by our lives that we love and honor Him above all else.

Xpand

Memorize

Today's Verse
"The God who made the world and everything in it is the Lord of heaven and earth and does not live in temples built by hands."

Acts 17:24

Read together Acts 17:24 from words printed on the chalkboard or an overhead transparency. Discuss its meaning in Paul's speech and for their lives.

Explain a rebus (representation of words or syllables by pictures of objects or symbols). Ask them to look for words in the verse that could be replaced by pictures. As they make suggestions, erase the word; leave the space blank or draw a simple line drawing according to their suggestions.

Give the children drawing paper and let them copy the verse, inserting their own drawings for the words omitted. When they have finished, they should know the verse.

Memory Project
1 Corinthians 13

While the students are studying the period that includes Paul's work in Corinth, they will have more understanding of the people to whom he was writing these words. As they memorize, encourage them to develop such love in their attitudes and actions.

Apply

Begin your mission emphasis with this lesson. Have your display on the bulletin board and/or table. Use it to give a report on the mission work to be studied. If the missionary sent a cassette tape or letter of greeting to the children, use it at this time. Announce the mission project for the offerings. Explain how the money will be used; encourage the children to bring in their own money—allowance or specially earned money. Enter today's offering on your offering chart if you made one.

Lesson Fourteen
Acts 18:1-22

Xamine

Acts 18:1. Silas and Timothy still have not arrived, but Paul crosses over to Corinth, a crossroads of commerce.

18:2, 3. Priscilla is evidently the Prisca of the epistles. She and Aquila became lasting friends of Paul. They all are drawn together by their knowledge of a common trade—tentmaking. Although Paul had been educated as a lawyer, as a Jew he had also been trained in a trade.

18:4, 5. Daily toil limited Paul's opportunities for teaching. The arrival of Silas and Timothy constrained him to a bolder ministry.

18:6, 7. Paul rid himself of the contamination of the very dust of the Jew's synagogue, as Jesus had instructed (Luke 10:11).

18:8-11. From this new base, Paul continues to teach, bringing many to accept Christ and be baptized, even one of the chief men from the synagogue. The Lord gives Paul special encouragement in a vision one night so that Paul is unafraid to stay there and work for a year and a half, certain of God's nearness and protection. During this time he wrote 1 and 2 Thessalonians.

18:12, 13. After this time the Jews rose up and took him before the Roman deputy Gallio, perhaps a man whom they felt they could influence with the charge that Paul's teachings were contrary to the law.

18:14-16. To their surprise and dismay, Gallio refused to hear them in regard to their religious discussions and threw the case out of court.

18:18. Paul takes Priscilla and Aquila with him when he leaves Corinth. Paul may have cut his hair because his vow had been fulfilled, or he may have cut it for the last time before the period involved in the vow. Such a vow was not an uncommon practice among the Jews.

18:19-22. Paul leaves Priscilla and Aquila in Ephesus. After preaching to the Jews there he determines to go on his way so that he can reach Jerusalem in time for the Passover.

Xcite

For this lesson teach two songs—one for singing in future worship times and the other for a fun overview of Priscilla and Aquila.

"Let Us Love One Another," page 105, will relate well to 1 Corinthians 13 if any of your students are memorizing it. Commend individual students and the group for any acts of love that you have witnessed in the past weeks in children's church or in the halls. A group action might be an occasion when they did not laugh at someone in an embarrassing position, or a session when they made a new person feel welcome. Use this opportunity to give positive reinforcement to your students.

"Two Hebrew Tentmakers," page 89, will help your students remember the Bible details much longer. If your schedule doesn't allow time to learn both songs, take a few students to another room to learn the song and sing it as a choir.

Xpress

Order of Worship

Prelude
"We Worship God," 104
Call to Worship: Psalm 145:1-3
"Happiness," 83
"Let Us Love One Another," 105
"Jesus Loves Me"
Communion
Offering
Introduction/Bible Story
Application Story
"Two Hebrew Tentmakers," 89
Prayer

Introduction

A picture portraying a vision will be helpful as you begin this lesson. If none is available, have someone ready to read a definition from the dictionary.

What is a vision? Allow discussion. *You will remember that Paul had a vision telling him to go over into Macedonia. In today's lesson he has another vision that gives him the courage to stay on and work without fear in this very difficult city of Corinth.*

God does not work in our lives in the same way that He did in Paul's. He does not speak to us in a

38

vision. There will be no direct voice to cheer us when we are discouraged or frightened or in need of guidance. Maybe we sometimes wish that He would speak to us so that we could hear him, right out loud with our ears. Yet He does speak to us. Through His Word He offers us the encouragement and strength we need for each day. The important thing is that we must know that God is speaking to us—each of us—that the Bible is not just a book to study, but a voice to hear and obey.

Bible Story

Corinth was a very wicked city. Coming there alone, Paul had to have considerable courage to begin his work of trying to reach first the Jews and then the Greeks for Jesus. It is not surprising that he was much encouraged by the arrival of Silas and Timothy. The Lord blessed their work there so that they were able to reach many for Christ and the special vision which He granted to Paul in the way of encouragement and strength shows His tender regard for our human need.

Use the map to continue the journey up to this point and at the close of the lesson, take them on through Ephesus, Caesarea, and Antioch.

Application Story

It's seldom an easy matter to move into a new community and it is especially difficult if you are shy, as Nancy was. She felt that she would never be able to make new friends. Back at home she had friends that she had known since they were babies together. But here she was all alone.

During the first week since she'd moved into the new house, Nancy had stayed by herself. The thing that was worrying her most was that on Monday she was going to have to start attending the new school near their house. Anyone who has ever had to enter a new school in the middle of the year will know how Nancy was feeling. If only she had even one friend she would not feel so sad.

On Sunday morning her parents began bustling around just as if they were still back home—getting ready for church. Nancy found herself feeling a bit curious about the new church, yet lonely and wistful for the one she had attended from Nursery age.

As the family approached the new church building Nancy smiled to herself as she heard the organ—one of her favorite hymns. "At least that's not strange or new," she thought.

When the service was over, Nancy and her parents found themselves meeting many friendly people. A girl came up with a friendly smile.

"Hi," she said. "Are you going to live here? Where will you go to school? My name's Anne"—

and before long Nancy knew Anne was in her grade, the friend she needed when she entered the new school tomorrow.

Paul moved into the strange city of Corinth. It was a wicked city, a very large city where a man could feel very strange and lonely. But Paul knew that when he found people who loved and honored God, he would no longer be alone. Aquila and Priscilla were believing and faithful Jews who were able to help Paul find work as a tentmaker while he was able to help them to know and love the Lord Jesus.

Xpand

Memorize

Today's Verse
"Praise be to the God and Father of our Lord Jesus Christ, the Father of compassion and the God of all comfort, **who comforts us in all our troubles."**

2 Corinthians 1:3, 4a

The words mean much when we recognize that Paul, who experienced so many troubles, was writing these reassuring words to the people in Corinth. When memorized, they should be helpful to your students when they encounter trouble.

Use the erasure of words method from lesson one to learn this verse. Primary leaders, use an ellipsis to show that words are left out when you print the shortened version. Explain its use to the children.

Memory Project
Are any of the children ready to recite part of the passage in worship next week?

Apply

Primaries: Review briefly how many different places and people heard about Jesus because of Paul, Silas, Timothy, Luke, Aquila, Priscilla, and others. Tell briefly about the people who are hearing about Jesus through the missionaries you introduced last week.

Ask the children to imagine that they are traveling with Paul or with the missionaries. *What would you want to tell the people about Jesus?* If necessary, ask questions to keep them thinking and talking. Conclude by summarizing their ideas and praying for the missionaries.

Middlers/Juniors: Complete Paul's second trip on the students' maps, reviewing events as they work. On a modern map, let volunteers locate the places where your missionaries work. Tell the students about any experiences or conditions that the missionaries face that are similar to Paul's.

Lesson Fifteen

Acts 19:8-22

Xamine

Acts 19:8. Paul is now in Ephesus, having started from Antioch (18:22) and revisited the churches established in Galatia and Phrygia (18:24). He again begins his ministry in the synagogue. This is Paul's third missionary journey.

19:9. This time opposition came not from synagogue leaders, but individuals who rejected the gospel. "That way" was used frequently to describe the Christian system.

19:10-12. These two years plus three months of teaching in the synagogue plus a brief time at the close of Paul's stay in Ephesus totals almost the round three years mentioned in Acts 20:31.

19:13. These vagabond Jews were evidently wandering "wonder workers" who went from place to place claiming power to drive out evil spirits. Having seen Paul's ability to perform this miracle in the name of Jesus, they determined to use that name, hoping for the same miraculous effect.

19:15, 16. The effect achieved was not what these false workers expected or wanted. The evil spirit rejected their right to use the name of Jesus and caused the man in whom they dwelt to leap upon them with great violence.

19:17. Both Jews and Greeks were able to see that the name of Jesus was not to be used in a careless manner.

19:18, 19. Having seen the example of what happened to the seven sons, some of those who had been working or experimenting with the magic arts came forward to confess this as sin. Many of them burned their valuable magic books that all might see the sincerity of their repentance.

19:20, 21. Having seen that the work in Ephesus was becoming well established, Paul determined that before long he would begin to make his way back to Jerusalem. For the first time he also mentions the wish or need to go on to Rome.

19:22. Paul evidently planned to take up a collection for the poor in Jerusalem and to aid in this purpose he sent Timothy and Erastus on ahead of him. Erastus was a treasurer of the city of Corinth and a wise choice to send on such a mission.

Xcite

The game, *Match the Mixed-up Journey,* will review the past few weeks' lesson for the Middlers and Juniors. Decide which form of play you will use: team, small group, or individual. Photocopy the number of game sheets you need from the game on page 72 and cut the game pieces apart:

1. *Team play:* divide the class into two or three teams. Give each team one set of the cut-up sentences. Let the teams race to assemble the sentences.

2. *Small group:* distribute a set of cut-up sentences to every three children. Turn all the pieces over; each child takes four pieces of paper. The remaining pieces are stacked into a draw pile. The first player draws the top piece; if it does not complete a half-sentence that he has in his hand, he begins a discard pile. The second player may draw that half-sentence if it will complete a sentence in his hand or draw the top piece from the draw pile. Play continues in this manner. When a player puts together a sentence, he lays it on the table in front of him and draws another piece. Play ends when a player has used all of his beginning half-sentences. The player with the most sentences is the winner.

3. *Individual:* each student gets his own set of sentences; cuts them apart and reassembles them to see how well he remembers the journey.

The assembled sentences are:

Paul stayed in Corinth for a year-and-a-half.
Paul and Silas went first to Lystra and Derbe.
Timothy's father was a Greek.
Timothy's mother was Jewish.
Paul earned his living in Corinth as a tentmaker.
The people of Athens worshipped many idols.
Paul always preached first to the Jewish people.
In Paul's vision a man from Macedonia asked for help.
Paul and Silas were beaten and put in prison.
In Athens Paul preached on Mars Hill.
Priscilla and Aquila lived in the city of Corinth.
Paul wanted God to let him preach in Asia.
Luke was one of Paul's companions on the second journey.

Teach the **Primaries** the prayer song, "Father, We Thank You," page 92. Explain that it is actually a prayer addressed to God. Prepare to sing it as a choir during worship, either as a prayer or to lead into prayer.

When the choir is ready, bring the games of the other students to an end and introduce to the total group a new song to use for the communion service. Sing "The Love Feast," page 103, once for the children. Ask, *"What is Jesus talking about in this song?"* Review the importance and the meaning of communion. Sing the song again for them, suggesting they imagine Jesus' talking to the apostles as you sing.

Xpress

Order of Worship

Prelude
"Stand Up, Sing Out," 93
Call to Worship: Psalm 34:3
"Let the Word of Christ Dwell in You," 84
"Let Us Love One Another," 105
"Father, We Thank You," Choir
Prayer
"The Love Feast," 103
Communion
Offering
Introduction/Bible Story
Application Story
"Come, Follow Jesus Wherever He Leads Us," 96
Prayer

Introduction

Bring an empty candy box to class. Ask the class, *Would any of you like to have a nice box of candy like this? Do you like candy?* and so forth—really build it up—then admit that there is something wrong with this gift. Let them guess what is wrong. Then open the box and show that it is empty. Point out that although you could fool them for a while, the time was sure to come when they would have found out that all was not what it seemed to be.

There is an old saying that says, in part "You can fool all of the people some of the time." What we need to realize and face as an important fact is that we cannot ever fool God. He sees and knows our hearts, even better than we know ourselves. Some people like to pretend that they are bad, worse than they really are; others that they are better than they are. We can be really thankful that God knows us, the real us, and he also knows what we want to be and can be with His help.

Bible Story

There is quite a bit of humor in the story of the sons of Sceva. False magicians who are put in their place and punished in such a dramatic fashion have gotten just what they deserve.

The important lesson to be learned from this passage is that the name of Jesus cannot and must not be taken lightly. The false ones tried to use His name for power or prestige or profit and they were punished severely.

It is exciting to see that the people of Ephesus understood that the name of Jesus was to be magnified and honored. Their actions in destroying the books of magic showed that they intended to have no further dealing with that which they now knew to be false.

Application Story

It wasn't hard for Johnny to fool his parents about his school work. Mom would say, "How are things at school, Johnny?" or, "Do you have any homework tonight?" Johnny just pretended he was getting along fine.

Of course Miss Grey, his teacher, was not fooled. She tried to send home notes to his parents—but somehow they never got there. They were "accidentally" mislaid somewhere along the way.

Surely Johnny must have known that this situation could not go on for very long. Sooner or later his real school life was going to be discovered, but he didn't bother to think about that.

Imagine Johnny's embarrassment when he came home late one afternoon after a delightfully lazy time of loafing around with his friends. As soon as he came on the porch he heard voices and one was a voice he did not want to hear—at least not in his living room talking to his mother. When Johnny's mother said, gently but firmly, "Johnny, would you please come in here. Miss Grey and I would like to talk to you," Johnny knew that he couldn't hope to fool anyone anymore.

The magicians in Ephesus had evidently managed to fool the people there for some time. Perhaps they had even fooled themselves into believing that they had some sort of special power or magic at their command—but they could not fool God.

When they tried to do miracles in the name of Jesus or in the name of Paul, even the demons mocked them saying, "We know Paul and we know Jesus, but who are you?"

Let's live our lives openly and honestly before God and before the people around us so that we need never be ashamed.

Xpand

Memorize

Today's Verse

". . . let your light shine before men, that they may see your good deeds and praise your Father in heaven."

Matthew 5:16

Use marks and embellishments to make parts of this verse stand out to your students. For example, underline the l in *let* and *light;* make glow marks around the word *shine;* make a horizontal arrow beside or above the word *men;* circle the word *see* and underline *deeds;* capitalize *praise* and draw vertical arrows beside *Father* and *heaven.*

Memory Project
1 Corinthians 13

Apply

Put emphasis today in this mission time on the members of your missionary family. If the family has visited your church, share memories of the visit.

In his letters to Christians Paul tells how much letters and visits meant to him. Give your students an opportunity to express support and encouragement to your missionaries. Select one or more of the following projects. Plan carefully with the children; begin your work this week and complete it next week.

1. *Write letters.* Give each child a piece of lined paper or an air letter to write a letter to someone in the family. Guide the selection process so that each family member will get about the same number of letters. To make the writing easier for Primaries you might pair them with older students. Suggestions for content are:
   a. Age and grade in school
   b. Name of school
   c. Author's family
   d. Pets and hobbies
   e. Something (s)he liked about children's church
   f. Special event at school or church
   g. Assurance that prayers are being made
   h. Favorite Scripture verse

2. *Make a cassette tape.* Tape the worship time of children's church. During this period add personal greetings and comments by the children. Favorite songs might also be sung. When you mail the tape, add a recording of the adult service.

3. *Send a party box.* Decide what makings for a party the children may bring next Sunday. (Next Sunday, box them up and wrap them.) The children might bring a cake mix, frosting mix, balloons, cards, canned nuts, decorations, candles, and hats. A birthday or an approaching holiday theme may be used. Check with the missionary to see whether duty costs on such a box would be high. If they are, send enough money to cover the cost of duty.

4. *Make greeting cards.* Handmade cards will be special to missionaries. They may center around a holiday, a birthday, or a "message across the miles." Used cards, magazine pictures, or wallpaper sample books will be a good resource for those children who don't feel artistic.

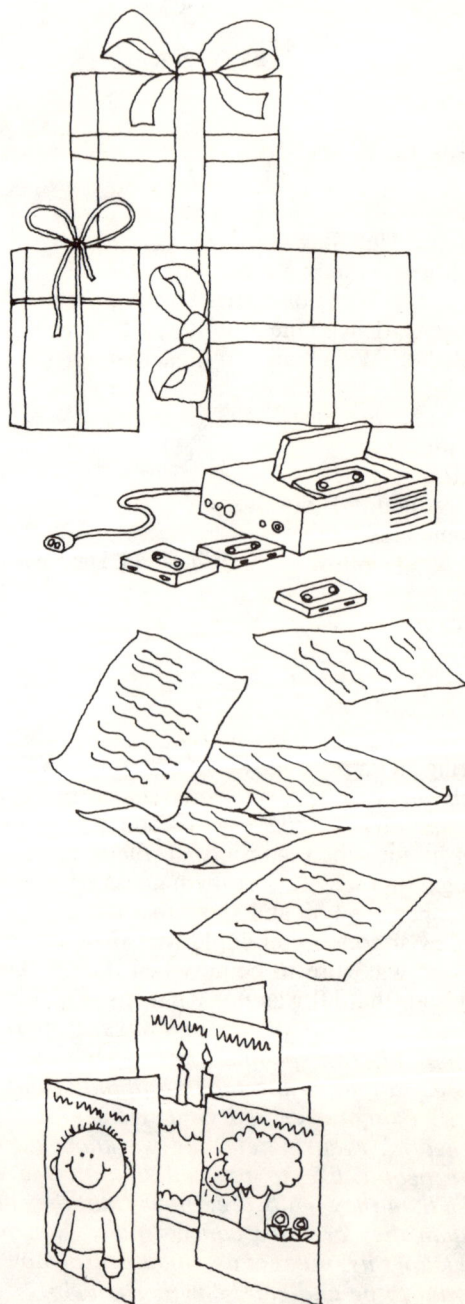

Lesson Sixteen
Acts 19:23—20:1

Xamine

Acts 19:23, 24. Paul stayed on in Ephesus for some time after Timothy had left and during this time Demetrius, anxious that his trade in silver objects of worship should not be hindered, stirred up trouble for the ones who followed the way of Jesus.

19:25-27. Paul's teachings were reaching not only the people of Ephesus but all throughout that part of Asia. In saying that gods made with hands are not real, Paul was causing a decrease in business for the craftsmen. The strongest argument that Demetrius uses is in a plea that Paul's teaching was turning people away from the worship of Diana.

19:28. Demetrius was a successful orator and rabble-rouser.

19:29. In the confusion Gaius and Aristarchus were the ones caught and accused as enemies of the worship of Diana.

19:32-34. Most of the crowd did not even know what all the shouting was about. The Jews, not wanting to be blamed for the uproar, tried to have one of their respected men, Alexander, speak for them but the crowd had no desire to listen to either the Jews or the Christians.

19:35, 36. The town-clerk showed considerable wisdom in handling the mob, appealing to their pride in their city and in their goddess. Soothing them with these words he urges them to do nothing rash.

19:37-39. Knowing that Demetrius and his group had stirred up the problem, the clerk tells them to take this matter up in a lawful manner if they feel that they have a case against Paul or these other men they had caught.

19:40, 41. He warns that they will, through this sort of uproar, cause Ephesus to be called in question by the Roman authorities. This quiet warning broke up the assembly.

20:1. Paul felt that now it was the time for him to go on his way as planned earlier (vs. 20, 21) back through Macedonia.

Xcite

The children will enjoy finding the message in the unusual Ephesus puzzle. (More than one letter will fit some blanks.) Make enough copies of the puzzle found on page 75.

Teach the song "How Much Do You Love Jesus?" page 94. Let the Primaries teach the rest of the children their prayer song, "Father, We Thank You."

Xpress

Order of Worship

Prelude
"Stand Up, Sing Out," 93
Call to Worship: Psalm 33:1
"How Much Do You Love Jesus?" 94
"We Look to Jesus," 100
"The Love Feast," 103
Communion
"Offering Song," 99
Offering
"Let the Words of Christ Dwell in You," 84
Introduction/Bible Story
Application Story
"Father, We Thank You," 92
Prayer

Introduction

Take a small statue or figurine to class.

Just suppose that I thought that this statue was very important, so important that people ought to worship it? Now suppose again that lots of people worshipped statues just like this one, made of wood or stone or silver. Pretend that you own a shop that makes and sells pretty statues like this. Many people come to your shop to buy, so many that you're getting rich selling statues.

Now a stranger comes to town and he tells everyone that this statue is not to be worshipped. He says it is wrong to worship any statue—calls it an idol.

How would you feel, Mr. Shopkeeper? Well, that's how Demetrius the silversmith felt; angry at Paul and frightened that he was going to lose lots of money.

Bible Story

Tell this story with enthusiasm. It has many facets: the angry merchants who covered their greed with a show of religious anger, their demonstration that whipped the city into confused action, Paul's desire to stand bravely before the mob, and his friends' insistence that he be kept safe.

When the tumult dies down, Paul is again compelled to move on but he leaves behind him many who have come to know and follow Jesus.

Application Story

Anna lived in Ephesus. All of her life she had looked at the beautiful temple to the goddess Diana and had been proud to live in the shadow of such a building. On her special shelf in her room she had a pretty, silver statue of the goddess. Her parents had given it to her on her eleventh birthday. How proud she was of being old enough to own this lovely statue.

One day a stranger came to town. As Anna returned from the marketplace she had heard him say a strange and disturbing thing. He had said, "You Ephesians are very poor, in your fine houses and big city, for you put your trust in a man-made silver statue, not in the God who made heaven and earth."

On a night soon after that, as Anna lay looking out the window, she heard a night bird calling and saw the stars shining brightly. Her heart longed to know more about this wonderful God of whom the stranger spoke. She prayed, "O, Diana, I want to know who made me; who made the world. Please help me to understand." But Diana sat still and cold in the moonlight and Anna knew in her heart that the statue did not hear her at all. She made up her mind that the next day she was going to find that stranger again and she was going to listen.

Many people of Ephesus felt just like Anna. When they thought seriously, as Paul's words made them think, they realized that the goddess Diana was not real. They were ready to receive the good news that there is a living God who loves them.

Xpand

Memorize

Today's Verse
"He answered: " 'Love the Lord your God with all your heart and with all your soul and with all your strength and with all your mind'; and, 'Love your neighbor as yourself.' "

Luke 10:27

Explain the context of this verse, including the fact that in Matthew Jesus, Himself, said that these were the greatest commandments.

Memorizing this verse will be aided by a combination of thought segments and pictures. Print the verse with illustrations on a poster as shown. Read the verse with the children several times. Comment on how the illustrations relate to the words. Tell the students to study the poster for a while, concentrating on each thought segment in turn. While they do that, draw the pictures from the poster on the chalkboard in their proper sequence. As a class recite the verse several times, using the pictures. Recite the verse several times with no aid.

He answered:
Love the Lord your God
with all your heart
and with all your soul
and with all your strength
and with all your mind
and
Love your neighbor as yourself.
Luke 10:27

Memory Project
1 Corinthians 13

During your work time today, help the students plan how to recite the sections that they know as an antiphonal reading. As they work out the details and try their ideas, their learning will be reinforced. Rehearse them so that they will be ready next Sunday to recite part or all of the chapter.

Apply

Complete the projects that the students began last week.

Review the facts about the family and the mission work that have been learned during these weeks.

Close with a prayer circle for the missionaries; if your group is large, divide into smaller groups so that all the children who desire, may pray.

Lesson Seventeen
Acts 20:2-13

Xamine

Acts 20:2, 3. Paul's route on this third journey is somewhat difficult to trace. Leaving Ephesus, he journeyed, probably mostly by sea, to Macedonia. Going through those parts, he spent much of his time in teaching and exhorting the Christians. He went down into Greece proper, probably in Corinth, where he stayed for three months. While there he wrote the book of Romans. Evidently he planned to go from there back to Syria by boat but a plot by the opposing Jews caused him to retrace his path through Macedonia.

20:4, 5. Here are named seven men who made up a part of the company that was travelling with Paul. Luke has joined Paul again.

20:6. The days of unleavened bread composed the Passover week, so they were traveling in the Spring.

20:7. On Sunday the disciples met to partake of the Lord's Supper. They were privileged to have Paul preach for them—and he spoke until midnight.

20:8, 9. This meeting was not at all secret, for it was well lighted. The window from which Eutychus fell was three flights up. He probably had worked all day and the lamps were exhausting the oxygen in the room.

20:11. Other passages using this word for "talked" indicate informal conversation.

20:12. The Christians were no doubt strengthened by this miracle.

Xcite

An adaptation of the game *Can You Think Fast?* uses your students' Bible knowledge. Form a circle. The leader who stands in the middle of the circle suddenly faces one of the players and shouts a name like "Solomon" and begins to count to 20. The person addressed must state a fact about this name before the leader reaches 20. He may say, "He was a king," or "He was very wise," or anything he knows about him. If he fails to answer in time, he must take his place in the center. Any Bible person or place may be used, and may be repeated during the game, but the same facts cannot be used twice.

Teach the song, "Gracious Father, Hear Our Prayer," page 106. When discussing the words of the song, point out that it is actually a prayer addressed to God. Use it during the next weeks as a prayer song.

Xpress

Order of Worship

Prelude
"We Gather Together," 97
Call to Worship: Psalm 150:1, 2, 6
"My God Is a Great God," 91
"Gracious Father, Hear our Prayer," 106
Prayer
"My God Is a God of Love," 91
Communion
Offering
"Father We Thank You," 92
Introduction/Bible Story
Application Story
"Come, Follow Jesus Wherever He Leads Us," 96
Prayer

Introduction

You will need a short piece of rope, a stone, and a disconnected light switch.

Today we are going to think about doing things that are different. Have someone hold the rope, someone else the stone, and another the light switch. Then, one at a time, tell them to follow your instructions.

First, ask the rope holder to pull the rope into two exact pieces. Next, the one with the stone is asked to squeeze it into a different shape and finally, have the one with the light switch attempt to turn the lights off or on.

Obviously some things just can't be done. They are either too hard or simply impossible for us to do. Yet nothing is too hard for God. Today we are going to think about a very wonderful "impossible" thing that God did through His servant, Paul.

Bible Story

This story has a really humorous angle. What one of us has not grown weary (for one reason or another) during a much shorter service than one that lasted until midnight? Poor Eutychus would have been wiser to have found a safer seat in which to doze. Obviously he had no intention of going to sleep! Of course the consequence was not funny at all. The believers there in Troas must have been greatly dismayed and saddened. Paul quickly tells them not to worry and with God as his help, brings this unhappy situation to a happy conclusion.

Application Story

Not very long ago there was a very sad report in the news. It told of a young boy who was drowned in an accident. His father, perhaps crazed with grief, felt that somehow he had a special power that would make it possible for him to bring his son back to life. He tried and tried, using every method that he could, to bring life back into his son's body. Everyone tried to tell him that it was impossible, that he could not do it, but he kept on trying. Of course he could not succeed and at last, exhausted and heart-broken, he had to admit that he had failed and allow the little boy to be buried.

Some things are impossible for us to do. God does not give you or me the special power to raise the dead or to work great miracles in His name as He gave to Paul and to the other apostles.

Yet we know that still today God does do wonderful things that are impossible for us to do. He hears and answers our prayers, sometimes in very marvelous ways. He gives us peace, He heals our broken hearts, and He saves us from our sins. Nothing is impossible for God. Because He loves us and cares for us we can trust our lives and our futures to Him.

Xpand

Memorize

Today's Verse
"Cast all your anxiety on him because he cares for you."

1 Peter 5:7

Discuss the meaning of "anxiety."

Bring in twelve shoe boxes covered with construction paper. Ask volunteers to print a word from the memory verse on each box. Build a wall on the floor or on a table using the boxes as stones. Let the children read the verse with the words in their proper sequence. Now scramble the boxes. Invite a

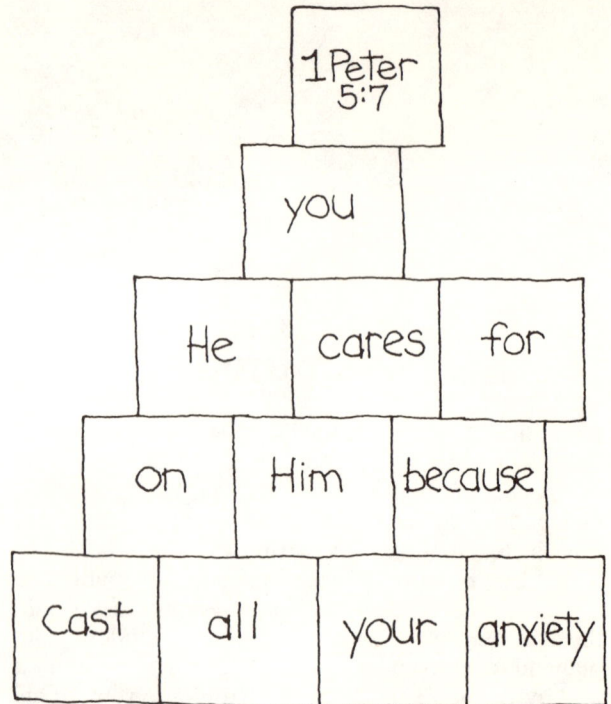

group of two or three children to try to rebuild the wall. Do this until each child has had a chance to help rebuild the wall.

If you prefer, you may use pieces of flannelgraph paper for the "stones" and let the students build the wall on a flannelboard.

Memory Project
1 Corinthians 13
During this last week of work on this project, let those children who have successfully learned the chapter, recite it for the others. Give recognition and honor. Would recitation of this chapter fit into an adult worship service in the near future?

Apply

Primaries: Make copies of the Who Did It? puzzle on page 76. When the students follow the directions they will find the name Eutychus. Review the story and remind the students of God's great power.

Middlers/Juniors: Distribute the students' maps and the colored pencils or markers. Again they need to select a new color for a new journey.

Guide the children in marking Paul's trip from Antioch through Galatia and Phrygia to Ephesus up to the churches in Macedonia and Greece. Using the double arrows, take Paul back through Macedonia to Philippi to sail to Troas (today's lesson location). As before, review the events of importance in cities as you work. This is an opportunity for the students to become comfortable with a knowledge of the geography and history of the New Testament.

Lesson Eighteen
Acts 20:13—21:7

Xamine

Acts 20:13, 14. Assos was a day's walk to the south. The solitude, fresh air, and exercise would have been welcome after an all-night meeting.

20:15. This route down through the islands off the coast of Asia Minor is a very beautiful one.

20:16. Paul seemed to feel that if he took the time to stop at Ephesus, it would be hard to get away in time for the feast of Pentecost in Jerusalem.

20:17. Yet he did not want to leave the area without meeting once more with the elders of the church in Ephesus, so he sent for them to come to him at Miletus, a distance of some twenty or thirty miles.

20:18-21. Paul recalls to their minds the three years of ministry that he had shared with them.

20:22, 23. In every city there had been persons who, through the Holy Spirit, had warned him that bonds awaited him in Jerusalem.

20:24. This verse is a beautiful testimony. Paul felt that no matter what trouble lay ahead, his ministry for Jesus had been worth it all.

20:26, 27. Anyone who rejected God's message would be responsible for his own eternal condemnation.

20:28. This is the beginning of a warning to them as the shepherds of the flock.

20:29-31. False teachers would be like wild beasts so the shepherds must be alert to protect the flock.

20:32-35. He reminds them again of his love for them and of his right to admonish them in this way.

20:36-38. Paul knelt and prayed with those beloved brethren and they embraced him, weeping because he said he would see them no more.

Xcite

The game that the children may know as *Musical Chairs* is also known as *Going to Jerusalem*. As you introduce the game, explain that since Paul in our study is on his way to Jerusalem, they will play *Going to Jerusalem*.

If you want to avoid any child's feeling left out, you may play this nonelimination form. As in the competitive version, music is played, and more and more chairs are removed each time the music stops. In this game, though, more and more children have

to team up together, sitting on parts of chairs or on one another to keep everyone in the game. In the end, all twenty children who started the game are perched on one chair—all winners!

Paul went to most of his known world. Teach the song "Be a Missionary," page 111. Relate the words to Paul's life and your recent missionary study.

Xpress

Order of Worship

Prelude
"We Gather Together," 97
Call to Worship: Psalm 103:1
"If God Be for Us," 98
"We Look to Jesus," 100
"Let Us Love One Another," 105
"The Love Feast," 103
Communion
"Offering Song," 99
Offering
"Be a Missionary," 111
Introduction/Bible Story
Application Story
"We Will Go to All the World," 110
Prayer

Introduction

Take a toy (or picture) airplane, boat, or train to class.

Have you ever gone on a long trip? Did you go by one of these methods of transportation? Show toys. *Did you have to go far away from people you loved? Most of us have—or will have to someday—and the hardest word we will have to say is that word "Good-bye."*

It was hard for Paul to tell his friends good-bye. It was especially difficult because he knew in his heart that he would not ever visit them or be able to see them again.

Yet he told them farewell and as he told them he went on to talk to them about some very important matters.

Bible Story

Paul's exhortation is very touching. He used all the emotional pressure at his command in order to make these church leaders feel the importance of his message. Since he knew, through the Holy Spirit, that he faced trouble in Jerusalem, He wanted them not to grieve for him but rather to be strong enough to stand firm.

Application Story

Andy decided to stay out of sight until the good-byes were over and done with. Then he wouldn't have to see people cry and get all sad. When his mother called, "Andy, Aunt Peg and Uncle Mike are almost ready to leave," he just burrowed in closer under the big tree, hidden by the branches that came nearly to the ground.

He heard suitcases being scraped and bumped about on the porch. Doors were opened and shut; forgotten items were found and poked into already full bags. The car was brought around to the front. Andy tried to whistle or hum a bit to shut out the sounds.

Andy hated for his aunt and uncle to leave. He loved them very much. They were moving all the way to South America and maybe he would never see them again!

Suddenly he heard voices quite nearby. "I just cannot leave unless we find Andy, Mike. I can't go far away without telling him good-bye," his aunt said. She sounded so sad and disappointed as she walked away toward the front of the house.

Andy couldn't stand it any longer. He wiggled out from his hiding place and raced after the two loved people calling, "I'm here, Aunt Peggy. I'm sorry. I was hiding."

Aunt Peggy stopped and put her arms around him. "Andy," she said, "it's hard to say good-bye—but sometimes we have to. There's one good thing about good-byes, though, for they make us want to stop in our busy lives and take the time to say 'I love you.'"

Paul's friends did not want to hear him say good-bye either. Yet they would cherish his words of love and concern for all the years to come.

Xpand

Memorize

Today's Verse
"Join with others in following my example, brothers,

and take note of those who live according to the pattern we gave you."

Philippians 3:17

Ask the children what Jesus' warning was in Matthew 7:15, 16, their memory verse for lesson three. Point out the similarity to Paul's warning to the Ephesian elders.

Today's verse sounds another similar warning by Paul to the Philippians. Discuss its application, especially the fact that we find the pattern to be followed in the Bible.

Memorize this verse through a combination of thought segments on separate lines and erasure of words from the board.

> Join with others
> in following my example,
> brothers,
> and take note
> of those who
> live according to the pattern
> we gave you.
> Philippians 3:17

Apply

In his sermon/speech to the Ephesian elders, Paul warned them to be careful about false teachers. The best safeguard against such teaching is a knowledge of the Scriptures. Guide the children in making a frieze (a series of related pictures on a long strip of paper—shelf, tablecloth, or butcher) or mobile that reinforces truths the Bible teaches about Jesus. Follow this procedure.

Remind the children of the warning by Paul and then ask them to name truths the Bible teaches about Jesus. List their ideas on the chalkboard or an overhead transparency. When their list is long enough for your purposes, write beside each item the Scripture reference where that information can be found. Teachers and older students should use concordances and topical Bibles to do this. Let younger children do the easiest or obvious ones that they know from memory verses.

If your time is limited or your students are all young, prepare such a list of truths with Bible references before the sessions and let the students look them up to see for themselves that the truths come from the Bible.

Draw a line through any facts that do not get a Bible reference. The rest of the list provides the subjects for the art project. Ask for volunteers (pairs, if group is large) to draw the truth on the frieze, or print the truth on a word strip for the mobile.

Lesson Nineteen

Acts 21:15—22:29

Xamine

Acts 21:15-25. Carriages in the King James Version means the baggage carried by the travelers. Paul is warmly welcomed by the brethren in Jerusalem. James, the brother of Jesus, was an outstanding leader in the church. The apostles were evidently gone at this time. James and the elders urge Paul to take action to prevent trouble from the Jews—to join with four young men in a vow to show his devotion to Jewish customs.

21:26-30. Paul agrees to this as a reasonable request but before the seven days of purification are past, the Jews from Asia catch sight of Paul in the temple, seize him, and stir up the crowd with the accusation that he has brought Greeks into the holy place. In a great uproar Paul is cast out of the temple and the doors to the courtyard are shut.

21:31. A cohort of a thousand men was garrisoned in Jerusalem.

21:32, 33. The Jews were going to beat Paul to death but when the soldiers and officers (several hundred) arrive on the scene, the Jews allow the soldiers to take Paul. The captain, thinking Paul must be some desperate criminal, binds him with two chains and then demands to know what is going on and who this prisoner may be.

21:34. The crowd answers in such confusion that the captain commands that Paul be transferred to the castle (barracks) where they are stationed.

21:35, 36. In order to keep Paul from harm, the soldiers carry him up the stairs.

21:37, 38. Paul's request to speak to him surprises the captain for he had not expected Paul to be able to speak Greek. He had thought that Paul was an Egyptian criminal.

21:39, 40. Paul identifies himself as a Jew and citizen of Tarsus which gave him status. Paul speaks to the people in the Hebrew language, the language they would know best.

22:1-21. Paul recounts the story of his conversion to Christ. His story is told beautifully and the crowd listens to him until he tells them that he has been sent to preach to the Gentiles.

22:22. Just the word Gentile sets the crowd off again and they begin to demand his death.

22:23. With gestures of great horror and disgust the people became a mob.

22:24, 25. Examination by whipping would be with the intention of forcing Paul to confess to some crime or other. Roman law, however, forbade the beating of a Roman citizen unless he had been tried and convicted.

Xcite

This morning play *Can You Think Fast?* (see lesson 17). This time, however, the person in the middle of the circle shouts another student's name. So if she said "Bill Jones," the player she faced must state a fact about Bill before she counts to twenty.

Learn a new offering song, "Give Unto the Lord," page 95. Tell the children to listen for how they should give as you sing the song. When they have answered, discuss "cheerful heart" and giving "as He has given." Remind the children that part of the money they put in the offering helps missionaries do what the second verse talks about.

Xpress

Order of Worship

Prelude
Call to Worship: James 4:8a
"We Praise Thy Name," 83
"My God Is a Great God," 91
"Happiness," 83
"Jesus Died for Man," 90
Communion
"Give Unto the Lord," 95
Offering
Introduction/Bible Story
Application Story
Prayer

Introduction

Bring a figure or picture of a cat to introduce this lesson.

Have you ever been blamed or punished for something you did not do? Most people have, at one time or another, and one innocent creature that is often blamed is the cat. When something gets broken it isn't unusual for the guilty person to say, "Oh, the cat did it." Sometimes it is said as a joke—sometimes as a way of shifting the blame.

Somehow that is not very fair to the cat, is it? No one should have to accept the blame and punishment for some action that he did not do. When that happens to us, it really hurts.

It must have hurt Paul when he was falsely accused of bringing Gentiles into the temple. He had tried to act in such a way that he would not cause any problem. He had been careful to have these men perform the rituals necessary to make them acceptable to enter the temple—and still he was hated and blamed.

Bible Story

In this story it should be explained that although Paul had been warned again and again of the danger of going to Jerusalem, he still felt that he must go. Yet he did not want trouble. He tried to behave in such a way as to avoid the wrath of his enemies, the Jewish leaders.

As is so often the case, angry men with unsubstantiated, passionate statements were able to stir up the crowd. The religious prejudice caused such a furor that Paul was taken prisoner of Rome in order to save him from the mob.

Notice that when Paul spoke to the crowd he chose the language to which he felt they might respond favorably.

It is interesting that the mob was willing to hear his personal testimony. It was not the story of Jesus that drove them into a frenzy. It was when he mentioned that the Gentiles were to be included in God's saving grace that the hatred and prejudice rose up against his words.

Application Story

Susan had not broken the window but it certainly looked like she had. It happened like this. Susan had been playing with the gang and had finally gotten up to bat. Her dad had warned her that the field her team played in was too small—that a really good hit might break a window or do some other

damage. Yet when she hit the ball she was not thinking about causing trouble. She just wanted to bring in the runners on second and third; she hit a good hard ball that flew outside and disappeared into a hedge.

No one noticed the two children playing catch at the end of the field. At almost the same time Susan hit her ball, one of them missed a ball and it crashed into a big window. When the houseowner came running to view the damage, there stood Susan, holding the bat (the two kids had disappeared). Before she had a chance to defend herself, Susan was marched out of the field, across the street, and up her front steps. The angry houseowner accused her in front of her alarmed and distressed parents. It took Susan quite awhile to explain what had really happened.

Susan knew how Paul had felt that day on the stairs as he tried to explain to the Jews just what his mission was, what he had been doing.

It is hard and sad to be blamed for a wrong you did not do. Susan was able to prove that she was not the guilty one, but no one would believe Paul.

Xpand

Memorize

Today's Verse
"Not to us, O Lord, not to us
but to your name be the glory,
because of your love and faithfulness."
Psalm 115:1

This verse fits the tune "Row, Row, Row Your Boat" by repeating the two phrases.

Not to us, O Lord
Not to us, O Lord
But to your name be the glory
Because of your love and faithfulness

Apply

Make enough copies for your students of the crossword puzzle on page 77. The Primaries will need some help. You may provide it in one of two ways: either print the answers (in scrambled order) on the chalkboard to help them with the spelling of the answers, or work through the puzzle as a group with the teacher telling how to spell the answer that a student supplies. When working as a group, skip questions that cannot yet be answered just as you would work a puzzle individually.

Lesson Twenty
Acts 22:30—23:35

Xamine

Acts 23:1. The chief captain who had arrested Paul wanted to understand just what Paul had done to make the Jews hate him. An appearance before the Sanhedrin should give the answer. Paul begins his defense by stating that his conscience is clear.

23:2, 3. Whited wall means a hypocrite, one like a tomb whitewashed outside but filled with corruption.

23:4, 5. Ananias was not truly a high-priest, but was serving in that capacity at this time. Paul had not intended to insult the man who stood in this high position.

23:6-10. Paul evidently knew that there was no point in trying to convince the council of his innocence. Seeing that both the Pharisees (who believed in the resurrection of the dead) and Sadducees (who did not) were in this meeting of the council, Paul raises the one question that will pit the two groups against each other. Placing himself on the side of the Pharisees, he finds himself the center of a great debate. The conflict quickly included physical as well as verbal violence.

23:11. The appearances of the Lord to Paul came at the times when they were needed most.

23:12-15. The plot shows the intensity of the feeling against Paul.

23:16, 17. Since Paul was a Roman citizen and had not been formally charged with any crime, he was able to have visitors.

23:18-22. The chief captain treated Paul's nephew with courtesy.

23:23-32. The captain formulated a plot of his own. With an armed guard of 470 men, Paul was to be escorted to Caesarea, to Felix, the governor. They would depart at 9 o'clock at night.

23:33-35. Having determined that Paul was from Cilicia, a province over which Felix had jurisdiction, Felix decided that he would try Paul.

Xcite

Play the game from lesson three to see how all the students are getting to know one another's interests and abilities.

As they arrive assign them to groups of four, ensuring that each group has an older student who can write. The members of each group should list facts about one of them (not someone picked in that lesson if possible) on a piece of paper. When most groups are ready, let someone from a group read its list to the rest of the students who try to guess the identity of the person being described.

Teach another missionary song, "We Can Reach Around the World," page 109. Tell them to listen while you sing the song and be ready to list the ways we can reach around the world. Help them select those ways that they have indeed reached around the world.

Xpress

Order of Worship

"Stand Up! Sing Out!" 103
Call to Worship: Psalm 147:1, 5
"Happiness," 83
"How Much Do You Love Jesus?" 94
"Let Us Love One Another," 105
"The Love Feast," 103
Communion
"Give Unto the Lord," 95
Offering
"We Can Reach Around the World," 109
Introduction/Bible Story
Application Story
Prayer

Introduction

Give every child, except two, a penny to hold, lightly, not letting anyone else see how much it is. To one child, give a quarter, or even a dollar tightly folded; to the other give nothing at all—just pretend to give something.

Have the children sit in a circle and explain that you have given them some money. One of them has a lot more than the others and one doesn't have any. Let them guess who has the larger amount and see if they can tell who has none. After a time of guessing, this might be a good time to take up your offering.

Usually it is fun to know something that no one else knows. For a little while each one of you held a secret in your hand—but it was a harmless sort of a secret, wasn't it? Paul's nephew had learned a very terrible secret and he had to decide the right thing for him to do.

Bible Story

Paul, the godly servant of our Lord, has been arrested and accused of something he did not do. Yet his spirit remains brave and strong.

Now, in prison to keep him from harm, the Roman captain doesn't know what to do with Paul. When Paul's nephew tells the captain of the oath—the terrible vow some of the Jews have sworn—the problem becomes so large that the captain decides that it is more than he can handle.

The secret plan to spirit Paul out of the city and away from the murderous Jews, the secret move by night under heavy guard, and the final safe escape make a very exciting story.

Remember that the Jews are left with quite a problem of their own. The vow to neither eat nor drink until Paul is killed is going to be pretty difficult to keep if they can't locate Paul. How can they get to him and kill him now?

Application Story

Sandy knew that Johnny had not taken the silver dollar from Mom's purse. In fact he knew exactly where the dollar must be. He remembered that when they'd heard Mom coming, Johnny had hurriedly put the purse back on her bed and Sandy had heard something drop and roll under the bed.

There was a family rule that no one was supposed to get into Mom's purse. Mom liked to keep it tidy, with her things in their proper places. But that morning Johnny hadn't been able to find his new top and he had gotten the idea into his head that maybe Mom had found it and put it into her purse.

Of course it hadn't been there but the two boys had found some pictures of themselves in a picture holder. When they had heard Mom coming down the hall they had dropped everything and gotten out of the room fast. Yet Mom had figured out that it was Johnny—and now her lucky silver dollar was missing.

What a mess he was in now! If Sandy told Mom to look under the bed he might end up with Mom looking at him as sternly as she was looking at Johnny. But it wasn't right just to stand there and let Johnny be blamed for something that he had not done.

Paul's nephew had a similar problem. It wasn't a safe thing to be Paul's friend. He might find himself in trouble with the Jews or even with the Roman guards, but he loved Paul and when he learned of the plot he knew that he must go and stand before the guards, tell them who he was, and warn them that they must help to save Paul.

How happy the boy must have been when he found that the captain was a kind and reasonable man. He knew that his courage had helped to save Paul's life—and Sandy felt glad, too, when Mom put her arms around both boys and said, "I'm pleased that both of you have told me the truth."

Xpand

Memorize

Today's Verse
"Be on your guard; stand firm in the faith; be men of courage; be strong."

1 Corinthians 16:13

When discussing this verse, ask the students for ideas of situations in which a person who loves God must "be on guard," "stand firm," have "courage," and "be strong."

It may help your students to memorize the verse if they remember that one *be stands* with two *be's*. Thus they will have their four verbs.

Apply

Use this week's script on pages 79 and 80 as an opportunity for all who are interested in acting to get a part. Let the children take turns being the actors and the audience. Each time it is read the students' knowledge will be reinforced. **Primaries** may take nonspeaking roles of plotting Jews, or pantomime the scenes as older students read the parts.

The chain for Paul's foot may be made of construction paper.

Lesson Twenty-one
Acts 24:1-26

Xamine

Acts 24:1. Whenever the Jews spoke of leaving Jerusalem, it was always referred to as going down, or descending, because Jerusalem is 2,400 feet above sea level. Tertullus is a Roman name so he was probably a Roman lawyer hired to speak for the Jews.

24:5. Here are three crimes; pestilent fellow (a person who corrupts morals), mover of sedition (one who stirs up tumults), a ringleader of the sect (this is a military term which indicates Paul was a principal person), of the Nazarenes (a name used only here in the New Testament to refer to followers of Jesus).

24:6-9. In the Jews' minds, this profaning of the temple was the greatest of the charges against Paul. They would have handled this under their own law if the captain had not interfered.

24:10. Paul uses the language of a man who is neither afraid nor embarrassed before Felix.

24:11-13. Paul firmly states that he is not guilty and he knows that the Jews cannot prove him guilty of any crime.

24:14. He is glad to confess that he is truly a follower of Jesus. The word for heresy is translated sect everywhere else in Acts.

24:18, 19. He makes the point that the trouble had really stemmed from certain Jews who had come from Asia and in reality they should have been the ones to come to accuse him.

24:20, 21. The council of the Jews could have no charge against him except that he had raised among them the controversy over the resurrection.

24:22. Not wanting to be forced into a decision at this time, Felix adjourned the trial.

24:23. Paul is not bound, and his friends are permitted to visit.

24:24, 25. Felix determined to hear more and his wife also listened to Paul's message. Paul speaks to Felix of those things he senses Felix needs to hear: righteousness (justice), temperance (restraint from a life of passion and evil), judgment (the time when all must account to God). Felix trembled for this message was directed to his needs, but he refuses to heed Paul's words.

24:26. Having closed his ears to Paul's message, Felix continues to talk with him from time to time as he hopes Paul will get some money and buy his freedom.

Xcite

In today's Bible study Felix avoids making a decision and taking some action. To introduce that theme and also learn still more about one another, carry out this activity. Sit in a circle(s). The leader begins by saying, *In our study Paul has made several trips. Let's pretend that we are moving to a new city and are starting to pack; we cannot take everything with us. We must choose carefully. Be ready to tell us two items that you want to be sure to take with you and why.*

Today's new song, "Spread the Good News," page 108, may become one of the students' favorites. When learning the words, ask them what the singers of the song will tell people. Use three groups as suggested for a pretty effect in singing the song.

Xpress

Order of Worship

"We Worship God," 104
Call to Worship: Habakkuk 2:20
"Gracious Father, Hear Our Prayer," 106
Prayer
"If God Be for Us," 98
"Jesus Died for Men," 90
Communion
"Offering Song," 99
Offering
Introduction/Bible Story
Application Story
"Stand Up! Sing Out!" 93

Introduction

Make four flash cards with words written large enough to be easily read by the group.
Maybe Tomorrow   Someday   Later   Wait
Do you like these words? That depends, doesn't it? Sometimes when you want something pretty badly and your mom or dad says (hold up each card) *it can make you feel frustrated or disappointed.*

But how about using these words yourself? Aren't they pretty convenient terms when you don't want to do something right away? Do you ever get into trouble by using these words?

In today's story we are going to see how a man used these words in a very sad way.

Bible Story

Paul is able to restate his defense in regard to his actions and "cheerfully" confesses his faith in Jesus and in God. Felix is well acquainted with the Jews and their laws and he refuses to take action against Paul.

Yet Felix is evidently a procrastinator. He chose to wait to hear the case till the Jews came from Jerusalem, chose to wait to make any decision until Lysias, the captain who took Paul into protective custody, should come down. It is interesting that Paul seemed to sense this in Felix for when he has the opportunity to speak before him and his wife, Druscilla, the message is on matters that have a sense of immediacy about them. He seemed to know that Felix needs to feel compelled to take positive action. How sad it is that even though Felix trembled at Paul's words he again said, "Wait, later when it is more convenient I will hear you again."

Application Story

"Sally, it's time to go to bed."

"In a minute, Dad."

"Sally, you need to finish your homework."

"Later, Mom."

"Sally, please run to the store for me. I need more eggs for this cake mix."

"OK, Mom, when I finish this puzzle."

Sally always said wait—unless it was something she wanted. Finally her parents reached the end of their patience. They decided to give Sally a good lesson.

The next time Sally was needed to help was on a Saturday morning. Her mother said, "Sally, please go upstairs and see why your little brother is crying and bring him down for breakfast."

Sally glanced up from the comic strip she enjoyed reading each morning. "Alright, Mom, in a minute."

Her mother said nothing more, just turned and went to get little Johnny herself.

It was a lovely, warm day and about 10:30 a.m. the sound of the ice cream truck came ringing through the air.

"Mom, Mom," Sally said, rushing in from her play. "The ice cream truck! May I have a popsicle, please?"

"Alright, Dear, in a little while," and her mother went right on sweeping the kitchen while the truck drove by and jingled into the distance. Sally was astonished. "I missed him, Mom!" she said indignantly.

In the afternoon Sally dashed in again. "Mom, Jennifer's mom says I may go with them to the park. They're leaving now, Mom! May I go?"

"Well, I'll think about it, Sally."

"But Mom, they're leaving right now—oh, look, Mom, there they go without me!" Sally burst into tears.

Mom put her arm around Sally. "Honey, it isn't a good thing to always say, 'Wait' 'Later'—is it?"

Sally looked into her mother's face for a moment and suddenly she understood. "I'm sorry, Mom. I'll really try not to treat you like that anymore—and look! They're pulling into the drive. They didn't leave me after all."

Xpand

Memorize

Today's Verse
"In the past God overlooked such ignorance, but now **he commands all people everywhere to repent.**"
Acts 17:30

Explain that although today's verse comes from another speech by Paul, Acts 24:25 would lead us to assume that Paul probably said words like these in Acts 17:30. Explain the words ignorance and repent.

To memorize this verse, show the two parts: in the past and now. An antiphonal reading will reinforce the contrast of the two times. Read and recite together until students know it.

Apply

Primaries: Brainstorm with the children the times or situations in which they often procrastinate—put off doing something. List on the chalkboard as the children respond reasons why they put off such actions. Make a second list of ideas for doing better at carrying out actions. Close with a prayer time, asking God to help them to carry out those ideas.

Middlers/Juniors: Make copies of the activity on page 78 for the students. Ask a volunteer to read the instructions for the Word Association and then the poem.

Encourage early finishers to write another verse to the poem or write a sentence describing the same kind of thought.

Lesson Twenty-two
Acts 25:13—26:32

Xamine

Acts 25:13. Festus has come to be governor in place of Felix. Again Paul has been made to stand before the Jews. When Festus seemed ready to do as the Jews requested and send Paul back to Jerusalem, Paul appealed to Caesar. As a Roman citizen it was his right to do so. In the interval between this appeal and his departure for Rome, King Agrippa and his sister, Bernice, come to visit Festus.

25:14-21. Festus explains Paul'e case to Agrippa, knowing that Agrippa's background as son of Herod Agrippa (Acts 12:1) and grandson of Herod the Great, would make this case of interest.

25:22, 239 Agrippa was indeed interested and the next day entered the place of hearing (courtroom) with a great display of pomp and splendor.

25:24-27. Festus again tells the details of the case; this time there will be many witnesses of his fairness. Since Paul's "crimes" were of a religious nature and should have been settled locally, Fetus is placed in a somewhat embarrassing position.

26:1. Paul knew that this address would not cause his release. He must have seen here another opportunity to proclaim Christ.

26:2, 3. Paul felt that it was a privilege to be able to present his case before a ruler who was well acquainted with Jewish laws and customs.

26:4-8. Paul stresses that in no way has he turned his back on his heritage as a Jew. Rather, he is now living and proclaiming the fulfillment of the "promise made of God unto our fathers."

26:9-12. He goes on to tell how he, too, in ignorance had fought against the name of Jesus.

26:13-16. This is the third account of the events on the road to Damascus.

26:18, 19. Here is a magnificent statement of the purpose and result of Paul's preaching to the Gentiles. As a Pharisee Agrippa would respect Paul's obedience to a vision.

26:20-23. Even though he is now in prison, Paul continues to obey.

26:24-26. Amazed at Paul's zeal, Festus forgot himself and burst out his accusation. The last clause of verse 26 was a common proverb.

26:27. Paul turns from this accusation of madness to a personal appeal to the king. He wants Agrippa to personally consider his own belief in the prophets and in Jesus as the promised Messiah.

26:28, 29. The exact meaning of Agrippa's reply is uncertain. He may have been speaking with a sneer or sincerity.

Xcite

As the students arrive this morning involve them in a game of *Who Is It?* (See lesson ten.)

Sing "I Love to Worship," page 102, for the students. Ask, *what does the songwriter love to do? Why?* Guide the children in learning the words and singing with expression.

Xpress

Order of Worship

"I Love to Worship," 102
Call to Worship: Psalm 105:4
"We Look to Jesus," 100
"How Much Do You Love Jesus?" 94
"Jesus Loves Me."
Communion
"Give Unto the Lord," 95
Offering
Introduction/Bible Story
Application Story
"Stand Up! Sing Out!" 93

Introduction

Write the word ALMOST in this way:

          A lmost
          L ater
          M aybe
     if   O nly
          S omeday
          T oo late

Today we are thinking about another sad word—probably a sadder one than the word we considered last week (later).

There's an old rhyme that goes something like this:

"The saddest thing in word or pen
Are the words 'It might have been.'"

Bible Story

Paul's defense before King Agrippa is famous for its clear and reasonable logic. It is also a beautiful testimony of his faith as he stands before this distinguished audience.

Application Story

One day a young man went out into the fields of his farm in the far north to take care of his livestock and to mend a fence that he knew was down. Some of his cattle had been wandering onto other homesteads and to find the break he had to follow the fence for a long distance. Just as he finished the repair job, a sudden, dreadful blizzard struck. The snow fell so heavily that he was soon unable to see even two feet in front of him.

Knowing the danger of being out in such a storm, he put his hand on the fence and began to follow it back in the direction of home. He was very careful to remember all of the rules he had learned. Keep the fence as a guide for as long as possible. Don't stop to rest even though it is hard to breathe and the snow looks soft and tempting. Once he did stop briefly but he forced himself to keep his eyes open for he knew that he must not fall asleep.

When he came to the point at which he thought the path led to his house, he had to leave the fence and begin feeling his way along, hoping to find some familiar landmark to guide his steps. Although he was trying very hard to move in a straight line, his tired feet began to take him in circles. Tired, completely exhausted, at last he could go no farther. He sank down into the snow, no longer able to care that this action would bring his death.

At the very last moment, just when he was slipping into what would be his final sleep, he felt a warm tongue sweep across his cheek. His big, husky dog had found him. The dog's barking brought help. He had almost made it home—only about 30 feet from his own door. Yet almost had not been close enough—it had nearly cost him his life.

Paul knew that for Agrippa to be almost brought to Christ was very, very sad. Paul prayed that "you may become what I am (a Christian)."

Xpand

Memorize

Today's Verse

"But God demonstrates his own love for us in this: While we were still sinners, Christ died for us."

Romans 5:8

Most of your students know John 3:16. Romans 5:8 reinforces the extent of God's love—He loves us even while we are sinners. Help your children to memorize this well. On those occasions when they feel unloved, unlovely, and unwanted, these words will give them comfort and strength. God loves them. Discuss the word *demonstrate* with them. Christ's death is proof of God's love.

Give the children index cards on which they may write key words. Let them select the words they will use; it will help them remember the verse.

Apply

Just as knowing Scripture passages can be encouraging, the words of songs can help your students. Gather them into a circle or semi-circle. Remind them of how Paul and Silas sang in prison. Announce that they will sing with you one of your favorite songs. Tell them why you like the song—a part of the words apply to your life, some of the words remind you of some truth about God or Jesus, the joy of the music, the fact that it is addressed to God so that it helps you tell Him how you think and feel, etc. After singing your song, invite one of the students to select a song, telling the others why he/she likes it. After the singing of that song, let the child pick the next selector.

Close the "singspiration" with any songs addressed to God.

Lesson Twenty-three
Acts 27

Xamine

Acts 27:1, 2. Festus sent Paul and other prisoners headed for Rome with the centurion (commander of 100 men) Julius. The pronoun "we" again indicates that Luke is with Paul. The last "we" section had dropped off upon the party's arrival in Jerusalem. Luke may have been writing his gospel. He is also accompanied by Aristarchus who is mentioned before in Acts 19:29 and 20:4 as being Paul's companion.

27:3-6. Julius treated Paul with courtesy, even allowing him to leave the ship and visit with friends at Sidon. Myra was the great port for Syrian and Egyptian commerce; it was due north of Alexandria. This ship was carrying wheat (27:38).

27:7-10. This was a bad time of the year to be sailing these waters and much of the time they were sailing against the wind, trying to stay in the shelter of some land mass as much as possible. "After the fast" would be in late September or early October, a time regarded as dangerous by the ancient navigators.

27:11-13. In spite of Paul's warning that the ship should remain at Fair Havens, the centurion preferred to heed the advice of the master of the vessel. When the winds changed they felt that it would be safe to sail on around the island of Crete to Phenice, a harbor more comfortable to winter in.

27:14-17. The term Euroclydon, or Euraquila, was the sailors' name for a violent wind from the northeast. Managing to run under the lee of the island Clauda, they brought on board a small boat and began to try to undergird the ship with cables or ropes which would strengthen the hull against the onslaught of wind and waves. The quicksands, or Syrtis, were shallows on the coast of Africa to the south.

27:18-26. For days it was dark and all aboard (except Paul) felt that they were lost. Paul reminds them that he had tried to warn them not to leave Fair Havens. Now he tells them to take heart, that the God in whom he believes has promised that all men will be saved.

27:27-29. Yet the storm continued in full force, driving the ship before it. The fact that the water was getting shallower as they took soundings confirmed that they were approaching land.

27:30-32. Color is pretense; foreship is bow or front of the ship. By cutting the ropes, the boat was lost but the sailors were kept onboard.

27:33-38. Meat in the King James Version is food. The number of people aboard demonstrates that the ship was a large one.

27:39-41. The rudder bands had secured the rudder so that it would not be beaten about by the waves during the night. The two seas evidently built up a sandbar on which the bow stuck.

27:42-44. Roman law was severe: a guard who let a prisoner escape might have to pay with his own life. But Julius took a chance to save Paul.

Xcite

A new game to help your students to be more aware of one another is *Back To Back*. Pair the students, telling them to stand back to back. As they stand that way, the leader asks questions like, "What color slacks/skirt is your partner wearing?" "Is your partner wearing glasses?" "What kind of shoes is your partner wearing?" "How long is your partner's hair?" "Is it curled?"

Teach the final missionary song, "Go . . . Tell," page 107.

Xpress

Order of Worship

Prelude
Call to Worship: Psalm 107:1, 2, 9
"We Praise Thy Name," 83
"If God Be for Us," 98
Romans 5:8 recited
"The Love Feast," 103
Communion
"Give Unto the Lord," 95
Offering
"Go . . . Tell," 107
Bible Story
Application Story
"My God Is a Great God," 91
Prayer

Bible Story

Trace the movements of the ship on the wall or overhead map. This is one of the most detailed and exciting stories in the entire Bible. Help the class to sense the great danger. The ship was not a huge vessel and it was heavily loaded. The storms of the Mediterranean are famous for their terrible nature.

Paul's courage and his steadfast faith in the face of such danger were a great witness to the heathen sailors and soldiers. They came to believe that Paul was one whom they could trust completely.

Be sure to end this story on a note of suspense. Although all have been saved from drowning and are ashore, they are stranded in an unknown and perhaps unfriendly place.

Application Story

"But, Mom, I don't want to go to summer school! I didn't fail *math! I just didn't do that great. I'll work harder next year, Dad!"*

All of Suzie's pleading did no good. Mom and Dad were determined that Suzie should get a good start this summer toward next year's math.

It was a sad and angry Suzie who marched gloomily into the classroom on the next Monday. Her summer was spoiled! She hated math! It was hard *and in her heart she felt that she couldn't ever really learn it.*

That summer there was a new teacher, a cheerful, friendly man who smiled and said, "OK, class, this summer we are going to discover that numbers are a lot of fun."

"Huh!" Suzie said silently. "Maybe for smart people like him, not for me."

From that first day to the end of the summer, Suzie never stopped being amazed. They played games. She got to help some younger kids who were having a harder time in math than she was. The fractions suddenly stopped being odd-looking numbers and became reasonable parts of understandable measures and shapes.

Suzie learned that although we may find ourselves where we don't want to be, we can do good for ourselves and for others, just as Paul did on that sinking ship so long ago. God can use us wherever we are, if we will let Him.

Xpand

Memorize

Today's Verse
"God is our refuge and strength,
an ever present help in trouble."
Psalm 46:1

This week's verse is another one to give courage and strength through the years to the students.

Either the erase-a-word method or key words on flash cards could be used. In either method it might be helpful to the students for you to point out that *r*efuge, *s*trength, and *t*rouble are in alphabetical order.

Apply

Distribute copies of the Stormy-Sea Puzzle on page 81 to the students. As they solve the message tell them to think of times that it would help to remember that God is their "present help in trouble." Invite older students to go up to the chalkboard and write an idea. Younger students or any others may tell a teacher an idea that he/she will write on the board.

When everyone has the message, let students read it together. Tie God's protection for Paul and the sailors into the memory verse. Read through the ideas written on the board. Distribute writing paper to the students; tell them to copy down on their papers the situation in which they need to remember this Bible verse. Recite the verse together and close with a prayer time. Sing "If God Be for Us."

Jan 17

Melanie 30, 35
Ashlee 6
Hannah 34, 40
Trina 60, 50
Gayle 28, 39
Todd 45, 26
Ryan 59
Jimmy 70
Jeff 43, 27
Marshall 85
Jamie 41, 55
Joy 41
Jerry 77
Von 34
Donald 32
Scott 6, 40
Brad 25, 29
Aaron 13
Penny 29

Lesson Twenty-four
Acts 28:1-10

Xamine

Acts 28:1. Melita (now Malta) is an island about 60 miles in circumference with 95 square miles of land surface. It is located about 60 miles south of Sicily.
28:2. The term barbarous does not mean that these people were savage or uncultivated. Greeks usually referred in this way to people who did not speak their language; they were people who said ''bar-bar-bar.'' Immediate lodging was impossible for those wet victims caught in early winter.
28:3. The poisonous serpent hidden among the twigs was no doubt lying quietly due to the cold but when Paul laid it on the fire he was bitten.
28:4. Evidently the inhabitants knew that Paul was a prisoner. They obviously believed their imaginary gods were active in human affairs. The word for fastened is common in medical writers.
28:5, 6. Seeing Paul shake off the snake, the on-lookers watched for Paul to show signs of poisoning or die very quickly.
28:7. Publius was probably the governor of Melita.
28:8. The English word, dysentery, is derived from the Greek term translated bloody flux in the King James Version.
28:9. The Greek word for cured suggests the idea of an attending physician ''treating'' his patients. It may be Luke was also involved.

Xcite

By now your students know twenty-three memory verses. Use today's opening time to review those verses. Print each memory verse on several colors of construction paper (enough colors so that there will be one color per six students). Cut the verses in half. Hide all the papers around the room.

As students arrive, assign them to teams of about six students. Instruct them to look around the room for pieces of construction paper on which are printed half of a memory verse. They will find many colors of paper as they search, but they are to pick up only their team's color.

When a team has quite a few pieces of paper, the members should gather in one place to start matching the memory verses. The first team to find and match all its verses is the winner.

Xpress

Order of Worship

''We Worship God,'' 104
Call to Worship: Psalm 34:3
''If God Be For Us,'' 98
''We Look to Jesus,'' 100
Psalm 46:1 recited
''The Love Feast,'' 103
Communion
Offering
Introduction/Bible Story
Application Story
''My God Is a Great God,'' 91
Prayer

Introduction

Bring either pictures or toy models of the following items: airplane, a tall building or mountain climber, spider (or insect), and a snake.
What are you afraid of? Some people are afraid of flying. Show airplane. *The very thought of going up in a plane terrifies them. Others fear heights of any kind.* Show building. *They want to stay very close to the flat ground. Still others fear spiders or insects,* show insect, *even the non-poisonous types. Lots of people are afraid of snakes.* Show snake. *Many snakes are quite harmless but still arouse a feeling of fear. Maybe Paul was afraid of snakes, especially of dangerous, poisonous ones like the one in today's story. Yet, no matter what, Paul went bravely ahead in the face of danger, trusting God, and God was able to use him and bless his work.*

Bible Story

It is interesting that the snake bite seemed to prove to these islanders that Paul was guilty of some terrible crime. Paul is first blamed as a murderer, then hailed as a god.

No mention is made of any of these people coming to know Christ as Savior, though some may have done so during the course of Paul's three-month stay on the island. Whether they were converted or not, Paul was able to show them God's power and tender mercy as demonstrated in the healing of his host's father. Paul continued to work for God in the face of shipwreck, snake-bite, and false accusation—and God blessed him for his faithfulness.

Application Story

Nancy Turner was afraid of the water. Ever since the time when she was a little girl that an older child had teased by holding her head under water, she had been afraid. Even though she had come up choking and spluttering and not seriously hurt, she had not been able to shake off her fear.

As Nancy's friends had gone on hot summer days to the pool and had jumped daringly into the cool, blue water, she had pretended that she preferred to dabble and play in the shallow end or to sunbathe. She had finally learned to swim in the shallower part of the pool, but she was still afraid.

Then one day at the beach, Nancy had to come face to face with her fear. She was sitting on the lake shore, digging idly in the sand, when she heard a frightened cry. Jumping to her feet she caught a glimpse of a little head and a waving arm as they disappeared beneath the surface of the lake.

Nancy turned about wildly, looking for someone, anyone who could help. No one was near except for some small children who were making a sand castle.

Suddenly Nancy forgot all about herself. Her whole being became filled with the need to get out there and get that little person to safety. Only she knew where the child had gone under and she struck out bravely toward that spot. Not until she was back on the shore, working to help the child to breathe again did she remember her fear. When the child coughed and began to cry, Nancy said a quick prayer, a prayer of thanks that she had been able to rise above her fear and conquer it. Like Paul, she had gone ahead, even when there was danger, and God had been able to use her in this wonderful way.

Xpand

Memorize

Today's Verse
"The Lord is my light and my salvation—
  whom shall I fear?
The Lord is the stronghold of my life—
  of whom shall I be afraid?"

Psalm 17:1

Primaries: Add a twelfth shoe box to your eleven from lesson seventeen. Again, let volunteers print each word from their part of the verse on a piece of construction paper to attach to the shoe boxes. Build a wall on the floor or on a table using the boxes as stones. Let the children read the verse with the words in their proper sequence. Now scramble the boxes. Invite a group of two or three children to try to rebuild the wall. Do this until each child has had a chance to rebuild the wall.

Middlers/Juniors: Print the words of the verse in scrambled order on corrugated cardboard or poster board. Place a paper fastener in front of each word. Attach a piece of yarn on the fastener in from the *The*. The yarn is now ready to be threaded from word to word. (Some words will be used more than once.) Make enough of these so that you can give one to every four or five children. OR, make it in very large scale so that ten children can watch as one child works the yarn either at his own knowledge or at their direction.

- The   • is   • stronghold
- I   • Lord   • and   • whom
- the   • my   • shall   • of
- light   • salvation   • fear
- life   • be   • afraid

Apply

Primaries: Discuss how the people (or their relatives) who were made well by Paul must have felt. Print the words they suggest on the board. Then let the students express those feelings through sponge painting. Such painting does not require exact details and is easy to clean up. One child might draw a happy face while another make a design of happy colors, and another draws a scene that he associates with being happy.

Cut sponges into rectangular shapes of about one-inch wide and three to four inches in height. Obtain clothespins, tempera paint, and liquid starch or detergent. To paint, the student will attach a clothespin to one end of a sponge and dip it into a mixture of tempera paint and the liquid starch (consistency of thick gravy). Tap the paint onto paper to make the picture.

Middlers/Juniors: Students will complete their maps today, including the places Paul will go in next week's lesson.

Begin with Paul's arrest in Jerusalem and removal to Caesarea; trace the route of the ship up to Sidon, along the northern side of Cyprus to Myra, west to Crete, down to the southern side of Crete along Fair Havens, west to Melita Island (Malta) north to Syracuase in Sicily, north to Rhegium and Puteoli in Italy. From Puteoli he will go by land to Rome.

Lesson Twenty-five
Acts 28:11-31

Xamine

Acts 28:11. This is another ship out of Egypt; it had on its prow the images of Castor and Pollux, two semi-divine Greek gods who were supposed to protect those who sailed the seas.

28:12-14. Syracuse was a chief city of Sicily. The 180 miles from Rhegium to Puteoli was covered in little more than a day. Just as at Sidon, Julius showed a high degree of sympathy in allowing a delay for fellowship with Christians.

28:15. Christians from Rome, hearing that Paul was in Italy, came as much as 56 miles to greet him.

28:16. Julius, the centurion, evidently influenced the guard in Rome so that here Paul was allowed to stay in his own quarters and not thrown into the prison.

28:17-20. Paul was permitted to have visitors. He requested that the chief Jews of the area come to him for two reasons. Paul took every opportunity to try to convince the Jews in each place that Jesus was truly the Messiah. Also, Paul wanted the chance to defend himself if the Jews in Judea had written and accused him of criminal acts against the temple.

28:21, 22. These Jews were dependent on hearsay for their information. They probably had refused to listen to Christian teaching even if they had the opportunity.

28:23-29. This time Paul had an advantage: the Jews came to him. The evidences for Christianity were studied and discussed. The gospel made its customary division between believers and unbelievers. The quotation is from Isaiah 6:9, 10.

28:30, 31. The book of Acts was evidently completed at the end of those two years before the tangle of Paul's legal status had been resolved. Even in prison, he fulfilled the preaching and teaching functions commanded in the great commission.

Xcite

For your relationship building today, select one of the games that has been particularly successful with your students.

Xpress

Order of Worship

"Stand Up! Sing Out!" 93
Call to Worship: Psalm 95:1-3, 6
"My God Is a Great God," 91
"Father, We Thank You," 92
Prayer
"Jesus Died for Men," 90
Communion
"Offering Song," 99
Offering
"We Can Reach Around the World," 109
Introduction/Bible Story
Application Story
"Be a Missionary," 111

Introduction

Take a few old letters and postcards to class.

Have you ever gotten a letter that made you especially glad? Here are a few that I have gotten—from (indicate senders and places).

Have you written to someone far away, someone you wish you could see, and had that someone write back to you? Letters cross the miles and bring people close. They may be friendly notes or thank yous, newsy letters or very important messages.

Paul used his time in prison to work for God. Not only did he share the gospel with his jailers and the people who visited him, he wrote many wonderful letters that are now a part of our New Testament. Open your Bibles and find the epistle (letter) to the Ephesians, Philippians, Colossians, Timothy, Titus, and Philemon. These are letters of encouragement, teaching, instructions, greetings, and sometimes warnings. Without these letters we would not know many things that we do.

Bible Story

It is not certain how long Paul stayed in Rome or whether he ever left Rome. He may have been put to death there in either A.D. 64 or 68. What we do know is that for the two years of his house arrest he used every opportunity to the fullest for the cause of the Lord Jesus.

Have the class follow this last part of Paul's journey. Bring them, with him, to Rome. Show them, again, how he sincerely tried to win the Jews of that great city, opening his prison-home to them and to any others who might come to him.

Paul's heart was with the many Christians in the many cities he had visited and in our New Testament we have some of the letters he wrote to them. How thankful we can be for the faithfulness of this great man of God.

Application Story

Do you have a pen pal? James had. He had gotten the name of a boy who was just about his same age who lived in Europe. Letter by letter he and the boy, Josef, had become friends.

Three years after they had begun writing Josef wrote to tell James that the country in which he lived was becoming more and more communistic. His letters did not come as often after that but both boys still felt very much interested in each other. When they could, they shared their ideas and their activities.

The day that James accepted Christ was a very important day in his life. When he was obedient to his Lord in baptism he wanted to let Josef know of his joy in belonging to Jesus. In the letter that he sent, James told Josef about his faith—about his decision to live for Christ for all the days of his life. He received a very puzzled letter in response— "Who was Jesus? What is a Christian?"

James tried his best to write a letter that would help Josef to know about the Lord; about our loving Heavenly Father who sent His Son to die for us all.

When Josef answered he said, "This may be the last letter I will write for a while. Persons who are communicating with friends in the West are watched with suspicion. Yet I plan to learn more about this Jesus you follow. Thank you for telling me about Him. Your message gives me hope."

Truly the message of Jesus does give hope and Paul was willing to share that message with everyone he met. Let's be willing to live for Jesus so that our lives and our words will be a blessing to those whom we know. Like Paul, share Jesus' love wherever you go.

Xpand

Memorize

Today's Verse
"I have fought the good fight, I have finished the race, I have kept the faith. Now there is in store for me the crown of righteousness . . ."

2 Timothy 4:7, 8a

Primaries may have trouble learning more than the first sentence, but try to teach the next portion which tells of the reward.

When one analyzes the passage, one sees four f's in three *I have* statements with a reward. Point these out; underline these keys. Read the passage together several times. Ask volunteers to tell you the four f's—then the reward. Read the passage two more times together and then begin reciting it together until everyone sounds confident.

Apply

Your students may have already used letter writing as a ministry tool by writing to your missionaries. Give them another opportunity. Their letters may be evangelistic or encouraging.

Evangelistic letters like James' letter in the story might go to a pen pal or a relative. Letters of encouragement might go to a minister, a teacher, a sponsor, hospital patient, shut-in, college student, military personnel, or church family that has moved away.

Primaries: Can dictate a letter to a teacher, prepare a cassette tape, or write simple notes with the help of words spelled out on the chalkboard.

Middlers/Juniors: Let early finishers go over to the wall map and play *Find That Place* quietly. They should divide themselves into two teams. One student (or a teacher) says the name of a city that Paul visited and the first member of team one points to the correct location. If he fails to find it within thirty seconds, team two tries. Score one point for each place that is correctly named.

Lesson Twenty-six

Review Lesson

During this study you and your students have become well acquainted with one of the great heroes of the Bible. Use today's session to reinforce that knowledge and allow expression of what they have learned.

The plan will work in this way: the total group selects events from Paul's life to review; each small group then prepares a presentation of that event through its medium. (Each group must have a time limit.) When all the groups come together, these presentations assume the importance of the Bible story of earlier sessions. The final sharing of how students want to be like Paul is the application time.

For a sixty-minute session your schedule would be:

1. Large group planning—presession plus 10 minutes.
2. Small group preparation—25 minutes
3. Worship and Application—25 minutes

If you have more than sixty minutes, add time for preparation. If you have a small staff, you may select just enough small group assignments for one per leader. *OR,* you may recruit special resource people for the one session. For example, an artist could help children plan what to put on overhead transparencies to portray action. A person who reads well could help a few students practice reading their Bible verses.

Large Group Planning

As students arrive a teacher quietly explains that the group under the guidance of another leader is naming important events in the life of Paul. When a good list is on the board, guide the group in dictating those same events in chronological order for the teacher to make a second list.

Describe what will happen during the rest of the session. From the chronological list, select events for the small groups to prepare. The teachers especially must be quick to determine which event lends itself best to which medium.

Remind the students of the media with which the groups will be working: drama, flannelgraph, over-

head transparencies, creative writing, Bible reading, and music. Announce how many students may volunteer for each of those groups and then allow them to make their choices. As a group fills up, let that group leave immediately to begin preparation.

Small Group Preparation

Bible Reading

This method is good for any event that does not easily adapt to one of the other approaches. And it affords the opportunity for the readers to develop this public reading skill that is needed among adults.

The leader should help each child select the verses that best summarize the event, help him find new words in the dictionary so that he both understands and pronounces the words correctly, and listen to the children rehearse.

If there are several children in the group, practice also how they will smoothly and quickly continue the reading.

Instill in these children a feeling of importance about their task of Bible reading. This is not an activity for those children who can do nothing else.

Creative Writing

There are several possibilities that you may want to use. We suggest that the most effective for a group with only twenty-five minutes would be for the group to work together dictating to the leader.

Let them decide which person in their event they want to be as they write a letter to a friend out of town to describe what happened.

A good beginning might be to outline the event on the chalkboard before describing specific actions and conversations. Keep the letter open for changes as you work.

Ask a volunteer to copy down the letter when it is ready. Another volunteer may read it during worship.

Drama

The age and abilities of your students may determine which form of drama you use: pantomime, tableau, or acting out the story. Pantomime will be your best choice if the children will forget the story or get stagestruck. One student can read the Bible account or the group's script as the rest of the children concentrate on their actions.

If your children are those who have responded well in earlier lessons, they should be able to act out the story by developing an outline and then carrying it out. If there is time, set up scenes, with a narrator to set the new scene. One child might also make signs to put on children who form the scenery.

Remember your time limit!

Flannelgraph Board

If you have used the Pict-O-Graph sets during this study, this is an excellent opportunity for the students who like to tell stories to use that skill.

Guide them in finding the proper pieces. On the chalkboard write an outline for this group's event. Help them match the pieces to the action and divide the story into as many parts as you have storytellers. (Some students might be willing to be silent helpers.)

Rehearse the story to be certain that your group members can stay within the time limit and feel confident.

Music

This group has the important task of selecting the songs to be sung during worship. Guide them to think about why they want to sing certain songs and then put them into an order for the service.

If any of the events on that list at the beginning of the planning time is described in a song, it obviously should be given to this group so that these singers can sing the Scripture song as its part of the review of Paul.

Overhead Transparencies

This group too must first outline its event so that it can plan well how to picture it on the transparencies. If you bought either of the sets listed in the front of the book, have those transparencies available to see if they will fit into the outline.

When the group has decided what should be pictured on each transparency, give an assignment to each child or pairs. Give each child (or team) a transparency and make available quite a good supply of nonpermanent overhead transparency pens. One or two damp sponges will be helpful if someone wants to erase a detail in a picture.

While the artists prepare the transparencies, the leader or an older student should prepare a simple narration to accompany the transparencies.

Allow time to rehearse once.

EXTRA ACTIVITY: Any early finishers in any group may be invited to test themselves with the review on page 82. Have enough copies so that those students who do not test themselves during the session may take the review home.

Worship and Application

Your attitude and leadership will set the atmosphere for this to be serious and meaningful. Lead from one song or activity to another with appropriate comments. Affirm good work by students.

Close this time of worship by saying, *Even though this study of Paul's life and work has ended, the lessons that we have shared will stay with us and help us to grow closer to Jesus. Think for a while about this question—In what way would you like to be Paul?* Allow time for thought. *Now let's hear what you thought. Who will be first to tell us in what way you would like to be like Paul?* Close this time of personal revelations with prayer specifically for the ideas suggested by the children.

If any time remains, allow students to recite their favorite memory verses or select a song to sing.

Saul's Trip
(Acts 9)

Follow the directions carefully. When all of the spaces are filled in correctly, some information about Saul's trip will result.

If Saul was a Jew, write a in spaces 2, 4, and 13. If he was an Egyptian, write i.

If Saul always honored Jesus, write j in space 1. If not, write d.

If Saul helped Christians in Jerusalem from the beginning of the church, write x in space 10. If not, write y.

If Stephen and Saul were good friends, write n in space 7. If not, write u.

If a bright light was seen by Saul and his companions, write s in spaces 5, 8, and 9. If they did not see it, write c.

If only Saul understood the voice from heaven, write i in space 12. If the others also understood the voice, write l.

If Saul obeyed the voice of Jesus, write c in space 6. If not, write b.

If Saul could not see for three days, write r in space 11. If he never lost his sight, write f.

If Ananias was afraid to go talk to Saul, write m in space 3. If he was never afraid, write k.

1	2	3	4	5	6	7	8	9	10	11	12	13

Fill in the blanks in the following sentences. Check your answers by using the code.

1. _____ was sent to
   2   1   18   14   1   2   1   19

   Antioch to visit the church.

2. Barnabas traveled to _____ to get
   20   1   18   19   21   19

   Saul to help him.

3. Saul and Barnabas worked in the church in

   _____ together.
   1   14   20   9   15   3   8

4. The disciples were first called _____
   3   8   18   9   19

   _____ in Antioch.
   20   9   1   14   19

5. Agabus came up from _____.
   10   5   18   21   19   1   12   5   13

6. The Christians in Antioch sent help to the people

   in Judea where a _____ was coming.
   6   1   13   9   14   5

A B C D E F G H I J K L M N O P Q R S T U V W X Y Z
1 2 3 4 5 6 7 8 9 10 11 12 13 14 15 16 17 18 19 20 21 22 23 24 25 26   Lesson 4

66

Find the Words Puzzle

Put the first letter of each numbered picture on the lines with the same number. The words will be ones you have learned recently.

$\overline{}\ \overline{}\ \overline{}\ \overline{}\ \overline{}\qquad\overline{}\ \overline{}\ \overline{}$
13 1 11 2 5   7 12 11

$\overline{}\ \overline{}\ \overline{}\qquad\overline{}\ \overline{}\ \overline{}\ \overline{}\ \overline{}$
4 7 9   4 1 6 10 3

$\overline{}\ \overline{}\ \overline{}\ \overline{}\ \overline{}\ \overline{}\ \overline{}\ \overline{}$
8 9 7 8 5 3 11 10

Lesson 3

67

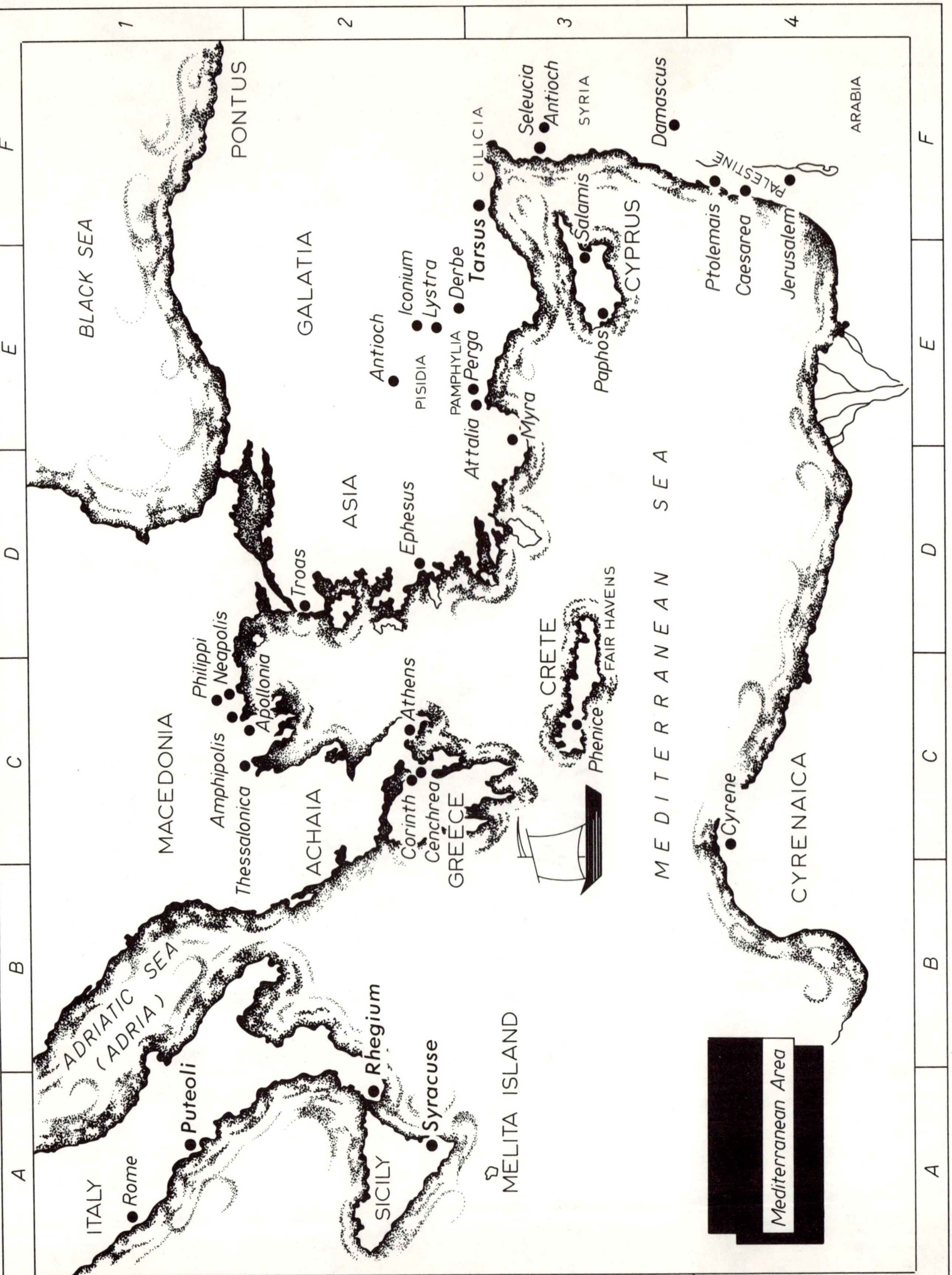
Mediterranean Area
A B C D E F
1 2 3 4
ITALY
Rome
Puteoli
ADRIATIC SEA
(ADRIA)
Rhegium
Syracuse
SICILY
MELITA ISLAND
MACEDONIA
ACHAIA
Thessalonica
Amphipolis
Apollonia
Philippi
Neapolis
Athens
Corinth
Cenchrea
GREECE
CRETE
Phenice
FAIR HAVENS
MEDITERRANEAN SEA
Cyrene
CYRENAICA
BLACK SEA
PONTUS
GALATIA
ASIA
Troas
Ephesus
Antioch
PISIDIA
Iconium
Lystra
Derbe
Tarsus
PAMPHYLIA
Perga
Attalia
Myra
CILICIA
Seleucia
Antioch
SYRIA
Damascus
ARABIA
CYPRUS
Salamis
Paphos
PALESTINE
Ptolemais
Caesarea
Jerusalem

Antioch
Go Ahead
One Space

Perga
Go back 4

Paphos
Safe

Iconium
Go Back
3 Spaces

Directions

1. Cut out the numbered pieces and turn upside down in a pile.
2. Select a button and place in Antioch.
3. Take turns drawing a numbered piece from the pile to know how many squares to move.
4. If you land on an opponent's square, he must return to Antioch unless his square is "safe."
5. You must draw the exact number to return to Antioch.

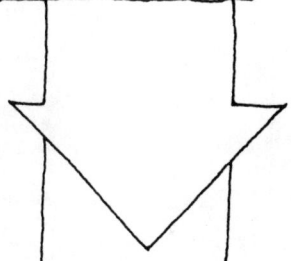

Safe

Salamis
Go Ahead 1

Lystra
Miss one
Turn

Antioch
Safe

Iconium

Go
Back
one
space

Perga   Attalia

Derbe
Safe

Lystra

ANTIOCH

1	2	3	2	1	5

3	2	1	4	1	2	3	1	2

PAUL SILAS AND TIMOTHY

END   BEGIN

_ _ _ _ _ _ _

_ _ _ _ _ _ _

_ _ _ _ _ _ _

_ _ _ _

MATCH THE MIXED-UP JOURNEY

Paul stayed in Corinth	the Jewish people.
Paul and Silas went first to	was Jewish.
Timothy's father	let him preach in Asia.
Timothy's mother	put in prison.
Paul earned his living in Corinth as	for a year-and-a-half.
The people of Athens worshipped	Mars Hill.
Paul always preached first to	second journey.
In Paul's vision a man from	Lystra and Derbe.
Paul and Silas were beaten and	was a Greek.
In Athens Paul preached on	a tentmaker.
Priscilla and Aquila lived in	Macedonia asked for help.
Paul wanted God to	many idols.
Luke was one of Paul's companions on the	the city of Corinth.

Cut on the solid lines. Get ready to mix and match.

Bible Drama I

Healing of the Slave Girl

Characters: Paul, Silas, girl, two or three owners, two or more men, crowd
Props: Any costumes that are available to make the scene more real.

Scene One

Setting: *Room with a table at which the slave girl is sitting. Her head is bowed. Her owners are seated nearby at another table with a money bag in front of them. Footsteps sound as a man comes to see the slave. The owners look up eagerly.*

Narrator: Our scene opens in a room in a shop in Philippi.

1st man: I have come to see the slave girl. I need to consult with her about an important matter.

1st owner: I am sure she will be able to help you. The charge is two pieces of silver.

1st man: *(Shakes his head as he reluctantly hands over the money and then approaches the girl.)* Girl, I need some advice.

Girl: *(In hollow-sounding voice)* What do you wish?

1st man: Tell me—if I go to Egypt on my new business, will I be successful?

Girl: *(Closes eyes and looks asleep. Pauses.)* If you go, you will lose all you own. You will be ruined.

1st man: Oh, that is terrible news! I must hurry and make other plans. *(Hurries away looking upset.)*

   (Owners drop silver in bag, shaking the bag so it jingles.)

2nd owner: Here comes another customer! This girl is making us rich!

2nd man: *(Goes directly to the owners.)* Here are my two pieces of silver. *(To the girl)* Girl, I need to know about my son. Tell me whether he will soon be home from the army.

Girl: Your son will not come home. He will be killed in battle. You must choose another heir for your wealth.

2nd man: *(Greatly distressed)* No, no this cannot be! *(He shakes his head sadly and leaves.)*

1st owner: *(Happily)* Look at all this money! And still others are coming. *(Crowd passes slowly by. Paul and Silas are with the crowd and they pause at the open doorway.)*

3rd man: *(Enters past Paul and Silas and lays his money on the owners' table.)* Girl, should I marry the girl that my parents have chosen for me to marry?

Girl: (Still using hollow voice) Yes, she will make you a good wife. *(Man leaves, looking happy.)*

2nd owner: *(Owners stand up and call to girl)* Come, girl, enough for today. Business has been good.

Girl: *(Stand up slowly and looks up; sees Paul and Silas. Her face stops looking blank and sleepy. Her eyes open wide. Pointing)* These men are servants of the most high God! *(Owners grab her and rush off stage.)*

Lesson 10

73

Scene Two

Narrator: Scene two opens on a street of Philippi several days later.
Paul and Silas walk across the empty stage. They begin to meet people as they go along. Suddenly the girl appears on the street, followed by her owners.

Girl: *(Points to Paul and Silas.)* These men are servants of the most high God. These men are servants of the most high God.

Silas: How strange and pitiful this poor girl is. She keeps saying these words again and again.

Girl: *(Still pointing)* These men are servants of the most high God.

Paul: She has followed us for many days now.

Silas: Yes, and my pity for her is great. Her owners care nothing for her except that she has a strange power and they are using her to become rich.

Paul: It is a great trouble to me. She is possessed of an evil spirit and she suffers. We do not want to be proclaimed as servants of God by an evil spirit. We must help this girl to be free. *(Turns to face the girl.)* I charge, thee, evil spirit, in the name of Jesus, leave this girl in peace. Depart from her. *Girl drops her pointing hand slowly. She looks at Paul and Silas, covers her face with her hands for a moment, then looks up at them happily.*

Owners: *(Yelling in rage)* What have these men done to our slave? Now she is just an ordinary slave girl. We have been cheated out of making lots of money! Throw these two in prison! They have robbed us! *The crowd closes in and Paul and Silas are pushed off the stage.*

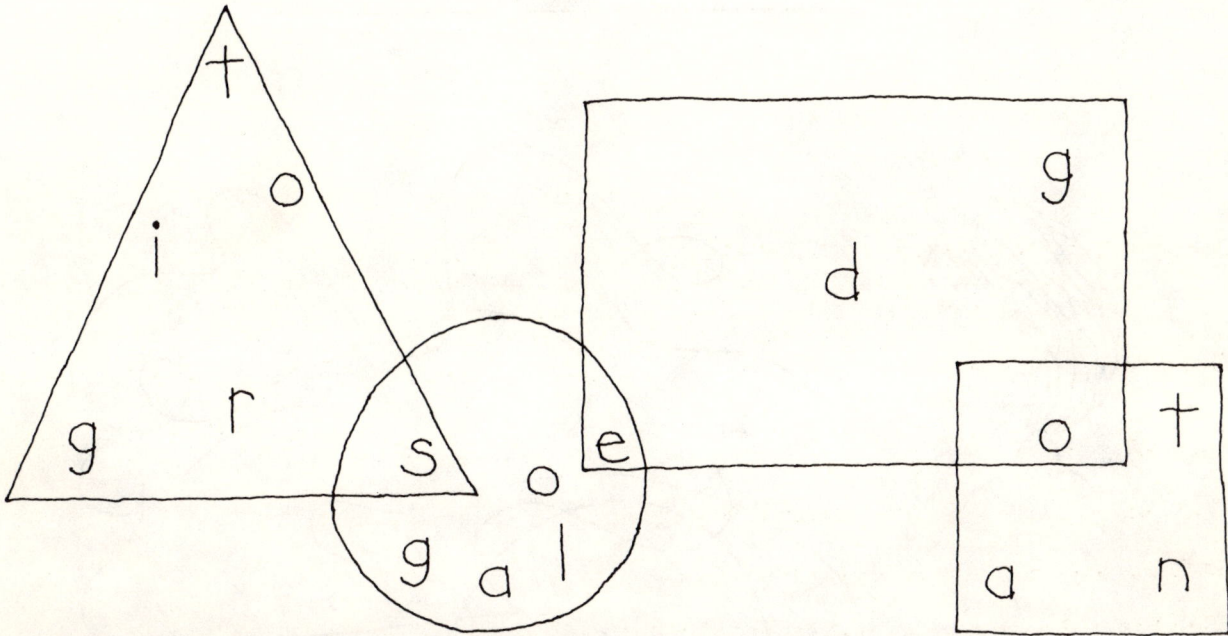

```
 1   2   3   4   5     6   7   8     9  10  11    12  13  14
```

Write on the line, the letter that is in the:

1. triangle, but not in the circle

2. rectangle only

3. square, rectangle, triangle, and circle

4. circle only

5. triangle and the circle

6. circle and the square

7. triangle only

8. rectangle and circle

9. square only

10. triangle, circle, rectangle, and square

11. square and the triangle

12. triangle, rectangle, and circle

13. triangle, rectangle, square, and circle

14. rectangle only

Who Did It?

Find the name of this young man who fell from a window while the apostle Paul was preaching. Follow the line from letter to letter. Print the answer on the lines below.

____ ____ ____ ____ ____ ____ ____ ____

START →

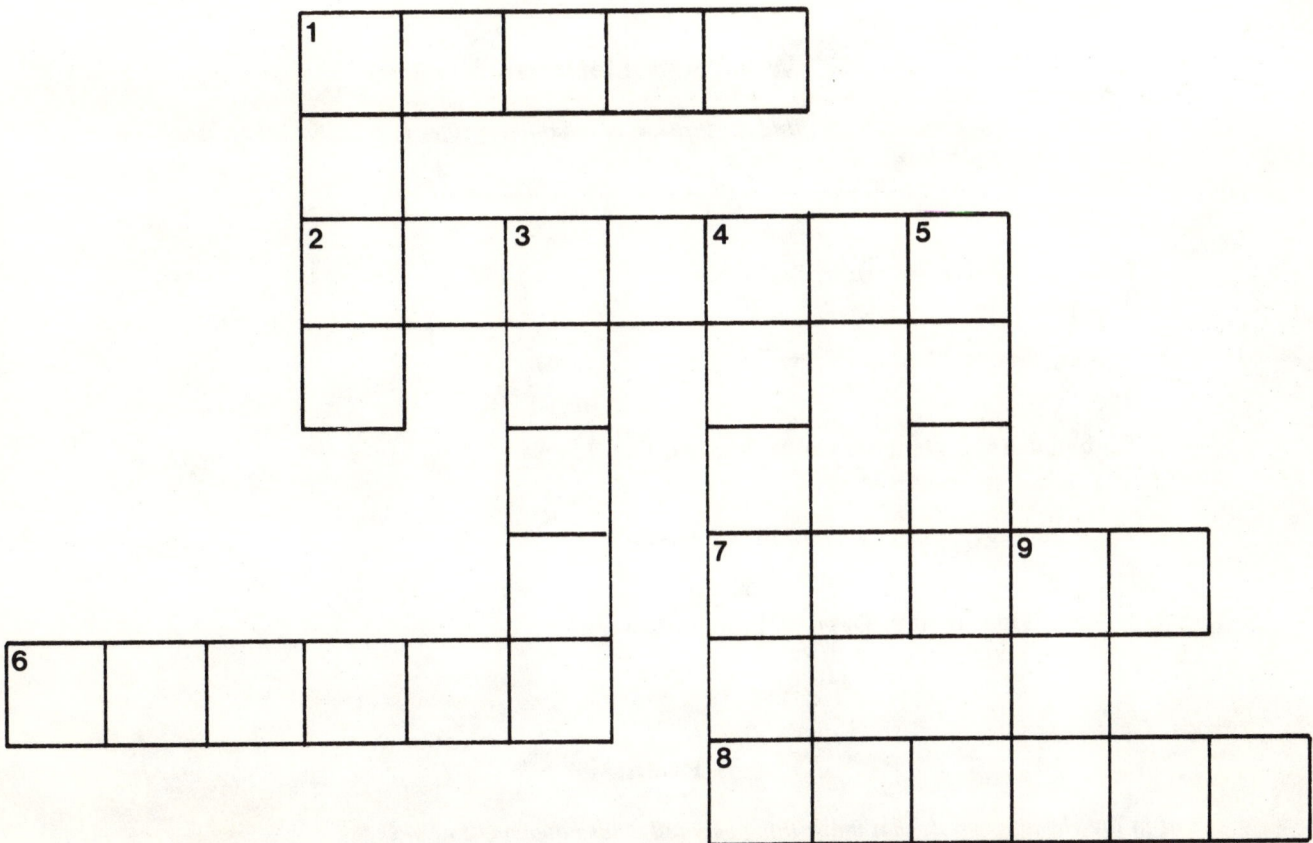

Crossword Puzzle

Down
1. The ones who accused Paul of bringing Greeks into the temple.
3. The chief captain was a part of what army?
4. The official language of the Jewish people.
5. The Jews had been trying to catch _____.
9. Paul knew that his life would not _____ in Jerusalem at this time.

Across
1. Paul wanted to be able to teach people about _____.
2. Paul went into the temple to _____:
6. The chief captain ordered that Paul be _____.
7. Another word for king.
8. The captain was filled with _____ or curiosity.

Let the Word of Christ Dwell in You

L. K.
Based on Colossians 3:16

LaVern Karns

"Let the Word of Christ dwell in you rich - ly." Let it
Let it be your guide when you would fal - ter. Let it

change your life and strength - en you with - in. "Let the
give you light when shad - ows gath - er 'round. "Let the

Word of Christ dwell in you rich - ly." Let it
Word of Christ dwell in you rich - ly." It will

lead your steps from sin. _____
bring you to a crown. _____

Word Associations

As you think about today's lesson, find the three words that fit together in each list below. Cross out the one that does not belong.

1. Felix, Druscilla, Governor, Bethlehem.

2. Prison, Chains, Paul, Andrew

3. Righteousness, Temperance, Judgment, Gentleness

4. Money-hungry, Greedy, Selfish, Cheerful

5. Honest, Trustworthy, Dependable, Foolish

Poem

Fill in the rhyming words that make this poem tell what happened to Paul.

Paul was thrown in jail that day

Because he taught of Jesus' _____.

He knew to serve he must be strong

To stop his preaching would be _____.

So Paul was brave and bravely tried

To tell to all that Jesus _____.

Though he was in darkest jail

His work for Jesus would not _____.

For Jesus loves us, this he knew.

He told the world that this is _____.

Bible Drama II

In Prison in Jerusalem

Characters: Paul, soldier, nephew, several Jews, narrator.
Setting: *Paul sits alone at one corner of the stage. He has a chain on his foot. Near him stands a soldier, on guard. Across the stage (as though in another location) is a huddle of wicked Jews. Crouched to one side, hidden behind a curtain or piece of furniture so that only his head shows, is Paul's nephew.*

1st Jew: Well, we have at last succeeded in putting that troublesome Paul in prison.

2nd Jew: Yes! And that should stop him from preaching anymore and causing us so many problems. Now his followers will be afraid to be as bold as he has been for fear the same thing may happen to them.

3rd Jew: Just imagine! Paul thinks that the salvation of God is for all people! We know that it is only for the Jews. We don't want him free to bring more Gentiles into our holy temple.

4th Jew: Prison will keep him quiet for a while but soon he may be released. You can't trust these worthless Romans to do anything right. They ought to have let us have him.

2nd Jew: I think he should be killed. He has given us great trouble.

3rd Jew: We must see to it that he dies. It is up to us to make sure that he is destroyed.

4th Jew: God would want us to kill this man who is a threat to our law. Paul must never go free again!

1st Jew: Let's make a vow that we will not eat or drink until Paul is dead.
All nod and murmur: Yes, yes.

2nd Jew: *(Looking around to make sure no one is listening.)* We must hide and lie in wait until Paul is taken from the prison. When he is on his way to be brought before the council we can make a quick attack, kill him, and disappear into the crowd.

3rd Jew: Come, let's go somewhere more private where we can sit down and work out our plan very carefully.

Jews leave. Paul's nephew waits a moment, then slips out of his hiding place. He looks all around to make sure they have gone, then slips quietly across the stage to Paul's cell. Once there he bangs on the door (or wall).

Lesson 20

79

Nephew *(Excitedly)* Uncle Paul, Uncle Paul! I must talk to you!

Guard: *(Holding up his hand to stop him)* Wait, young man! What business have you here? Go home to your mother. The hour is late.

Paul: *(Standing, but unable to move because of chains)* Please, Guard. This young man is my nephew. May I not speak to him? *(To nephew)* What is it, Son? Is there trouble at home?

Nephew: No, not at home, but there is trouble. I just overheard some wicked men making a vow and a terrible plan to kill you. I am so frightened for you.

Paul: Tell me about it. Don't be frightened.

Nephew: The men vowed that they would kill you when you are taken from the prison. They hate you and they have vowed not to eat or drink until you are dead!

Guard: *(Grunts in disgust)* Then perhaps they will starve to death—and good riddance to them!

Paul: *(To nephew)* You were brave and wise to come to me with this story. Guard, please take my nephew to the commander so that he may tell what he has seen and heard.

Guard: Come along, young man. The commander may not believe you—but we shall see. Perhaps you have saved your uncle from harm.

Narrator: The commander did believe the boy and moved Paul secretly at night to Caesarea. Guarded by a large party of soldiers, Paul was safe and the Jews could do him no harm. God intended that Paul should have more time in which he would live and tell others about Jesus. He used this young man to save Paul's life.

Stormy Sea Puzzle

The stormy sea below provides some information about Paul if you write down every second letter.

DQPdDiGKDEi;GiDEbENOFfOHPHOKSCWNRZOVLXTIKWAVSYEIHbTPVdPKbLgEOOHmowlTEKEILiBIAGAyaOSfwyOGjdUCaOBd

Test Yourself

True or False

1. _____ Paul was a Gentile.

2. _____ Paul was first called Saul.

3. _____ Jesus never spoke to Saul. (or Paul)

4. _____ The Jews trusted and helped Paul in his work.

5. _____ Paul was stoned for his faith.

6. _____ Paul never stayed in one place for more than three months.

7. _____ Diana was the name of a false goddess.

8. _____ Luke wrote the book of Acts.

9. _____ Paul said many would die in the shipwreck.

10. _____ When Paul was arrested he stopped preaching.

11. _____ Paul may have been killed in Rome.

Multiple choice (Circle the right word.)

1. Bar-Jesus (Elymas) was a *prophet, preacher, magician.*

2. The people in Lystra wanted to worship Paul as a *hero, brave man, god.*

3. Paul didn't want to take *Luke, John Mark, Silas* on the 2nd journey.

4. When Timothy travelled with Paul he was very *sick, bad, young.*

5. The Holy Spirit did not permit Paul to go to preach in *Africa, Asia, Australia.*

6. *Lydia, Diana, Priscilla* met Paul at a riverside prayer meeting.

7. In the Philippian jail Paul and Silas *cried, slept, sang praises.*

8. Paul saw many *lakes, idols, hills* in Athens.

9. Priscilla and Aquila were *doctors, merchants, tentmakers.*

10. Paul's *nephew, cousin, brother* warned Paul of the plot against his life.

Happiness

L.K.

LaVern Karns

1. Hap - pi - ness is hav - ing Christ with - in, Christ with - in,
2. Hap - pi - ness is liv - ing Je - sus' way, Je - sus' way,
3. Hap - pi - ness is serv - ing Christ our Lord, Christ our Lord,

Christ with - in. Hap - pi - ness is hav - ing
Je - sus' way. Hap - pi - ness is liv - ing
Christ our Lord. Hap - pi - ness is serv - ing

Christ with - in, And know - ing that we're free from all our sin.
Je - sus' way In all we think, in all we do or say.
Christ our Lord, And trust - ing dai - ly in His ho - ly Word.

We Praise Thy Name

(A Round)

For health and strength and all things good we praise Thy Name, O Lord!

Stephen

M. K. B.

Mary Kay Bottens

Ste-phen was a man Full of faith and power.

Ste-phen loved the Lord E - ven in his dark - est hour.

Ste-phen preached to men, But their hearts were full of sin. And they

stoned him, They stoned this man of God.

Beyond Jerusalem

R. B.

Ramona Brown

86

Down the Damascus Wall

J. L. H.

Jenna Lusby Houp

1. Paul loved Je-sus Christ his Lord, Trust-ed Him each day;
2. E-vil men de-cid-ed to Kill him if they could,
3. Trapped in-side the cit-y wall, Paul es-caped that night.
4. Paul was safe-ly on his way When the men caught on;

Trav-eled 'round to preach the Word; He fol-lowed in the way.
Catch him at the cit-y gate, Be rid of him for good.
In a bas-ket held by all His friends, he made his flight.
He would not be hin-dered as He preached a-bout God's Son.

CHORUS (*Use only after 3rd and 4th stanzas*)

Down, down, down in a bas-ket, Down the Da-mas-cus wall.

Paul and Silas

M. K. B.

Mary Kay Bottens

1. Paul and Si - las were in jail, __ They sang hymns and prayed. __
2. "What must I do to be saved?" Then the jail - er cried. __

Then an earth-quake loosed their bonds; The jail-er was a - fraid. __
"Come, be - lieve on Je - sus Christ," Bold - ly they re - plied. __

"Keep - er! Keep - er!" Paul cried out, __ "Do your-self no harm. __
Then they spoke God's Word to him __ And his fam - i - ly; ___

"We're still here in - side the jail; __ Please don't be a - larmed."
They bap-tized them all that night, Be - liev-ing hap-pi - ly. ___

Two Hebrew Tentmakers

L.K.

LaVern Karns

1. Two He - brew tent - mak - ers driv - en from Rome
2. One was a la - dy, Pris - cil - la by name,

Went in - to Cor - inth to find a new home.
Wife of A - qui - la___ We know of their fame.

There they met Paul and la - bored with him,
Once to their home, A - pol - los was brought.

Help - ing to turn man from dark - ness and sin.
There he the glo - ri - ous gos - pel was taught.

Jesus Died for Men

B. L. H.

Barbara Le Hays

Upon a cross, upon a hill, Jesus died for men. The mob with hate had shouted, "Kill!" Jesus died for men. Though pain and mighty sorrow had pierced Him through and through, He prayed, "Father, forgive them, they know not what they do!" Oh, love unending, love divine, Jesus died for men, Salvation brought to all mankind, Jesus died for men, Jesus died for men.

My God Is a Great God

S.B.S.

Stella B. Stack

Lyrics:

My God is a great God, A great God is He.

1. Who made the heav-ens and the earth____ Then the__ deep__ blue sea.
2. Who placed the moon and stars for night,____ Day's sun to shine up-on me.
3. He sent His Son from Heav'n a-bove, That I from my sins might be free. A

great big won-der-ful, mar-vel-ous God, Oh, my God is a

great God, A great God is He.

Father, We Thank You

Rebecca J. Weston

D. Batchellor

1. Fa - ther, we thank You for the night,
2. Help us to do the things we should,

And for the pleas - ant morn - ing light; For rest and food and
To be to oth - ers kind and good; In all we do in

Stand Up! Sing Out!

M. K. B.

Mary Kay Bottens

Stand up! Sing out! Shout, Hal - le - lu - jah! ____ Shout, Hal - le - lu - jah, chil - dren,

Praise ___ the Lord! ___ Christ is com - ing, Just as He pro - mised, ___

Just as He pro - mised In His ho - ly Word. ___ Com - ing in pow'r and glo - ry—

Oh, what a won - drous sto - ry! Je - sus is com - ing! Praise His ho - ly Name! ___

How Much Do You Love My Jesus?

M. K. B.

Mary Kay Bottens

Lyrics:
How much do you love? How much do you love? How much do you love my Je-sus? How much do you love? How much do you love? How much do you love my Lord? How much do you love? How much do you love? How much do you love my Je-sus? How much do you love? How much do you love? How much do you love my Lord?

Do you love Him high as the high-est moun-tain? Deep as the deep-est sea? Do you love Him wide as the wid-est o-cean? That's how He loves me! How

(1) Stand and lift arms high   (2) Lean over and touch floor   (3) Spread arms wide   (4) Point to Heaven   (5) Point to self

Give Unto the Lord

L. K.

LaVern Karns

Give un-to the Lord with a cheer-ful heart, Give as He has giv-en un-to thee._____ Give un-to the Lord with a cheer-ful heart; This is what my Sav-ior teach-es me._____

Come, Follow Jesus Wherever He Leads Us

Mary Kay Bottens

Traditional "Chopsticks"

Come, fol-low Je-sus, wher-ev-er He leads us, Come, lis-ten to

Je-sus, His Word ev-er feeds us! At home or at play, there is

no bet-ter way To be hap-py each day than to fol-low Him!

He is our dear-est friend, And we can de-pend on

Him ev-'ry-day! _____ He cares for you and

me, And He came to be Our Sav - ior to - day!____

We Gather Together

Stanza 1, adapted by Dorothy F. Poulton
Stanza 2, by Anna G. Whitmore

Ancient Dutch Folk Song

1. We gath - er to - geth - er to ask the Lord's bless - ing, He
2. We pray to our Fa - ther when night is de - scend - ing, When

loves us and leads us His will to make known. We
morn - ing is break - ing we sing to His praise. With

love Him and serve Him, praise and thanks we're bring - ing, Sing
wis - dom and love and kind - ness nev - er end - ing, He

prais - es to His name, He for - gets not His own.
guards us and pro - tects us and ____ guides all our ways.

If God Be for Us

M. F.

Mark Fessler

If God be for us, Who can be a-gainst us?

Who shall sep-a-rate us From the love of Christ?

Per-se-cu-tion and dis-tress, Hun-ger, dan-ger, sword?

None of these can harm us, If we love the Lord!

Offering Song

D. J. O.

Doris J. Owens

I'm bring-ing my off - 'ring, Dear Je-sus, to You, ____ ____ Be - cause You have told me Your work I must do. ____ ____ That oth-ers may know You, I'm giv-ing my part. ____ I bring it with love And with joy in my heart.

99

We Look to Jesus

Lois Morse

L. M.

We look to Je - sus,___ We let Him lead us.___ He is the

Life, the Truth,___ The on - ly Way.___ Come, walk with

Je - sus,___ Go where He leads us,___ Till we reach Heav-en's gates,___

Lyrics:

For-ev-er to stay! ____ We look to Je - sus, ____ Our Lord who shows the way; ____ So let's be faith - ful, ____ And serve Him ev-'ry day. ____ Come, let us live for Him, ____ Yes, e-ven die for Him; ____ Give heart and soul to Him, ____ For-ev-er - more! ____

I Love to Worship

P. H.

Patricia Hetrick

March time

I love to wor-ship, to pray, and to sing! I love to

wor-ship my Re-deem-er and my King! Gra-cious, for-giv-ing, so

1.

wise and true is He! His Hand will guide me Thro' all e-ter-ni-

2.

ty (And that's why) His love will an-swer my ev-'ry need and care.

Glad-ly I'll serve Him, and wit-ness ev-'ry-where.

The Love Feast

From Luke 22:19,20

Norman L. Starks

"Take, eat; this is my bod - y," The Lord com-mand-ed them.

"Drink the cup, this is my blood; Which is shed for all your sin.

As you take this feast of love, This do in re-mem-brance of me.

Love each oth - er as I've loved, Now and e-ter-nal-ly."

We Worship God

N. L. S.

Norman L. Starks

We will wor-ship God a-bove, Great and ho-ly is His love;

Let the peo-ple sing His praise, Let them all their voic-es raise!

Lord of Lords and King of Kings, This the mes-sage the

heav-ens sing! Till the sun and stars grow dim,

Bb Bbaug Eb F#dim7 Gm F#dim7 Gm F#dim7   Bb   F7   Bb

We will join our hearts and hands and   wor - ship   Him!

Let Us Love One Another

N. L. S.

Norman L. Starks

G

A7

Let us   love one an-oth-er,   Love one an-oth-er,

D7

G Fdim7 D7

G

Grow-ing and car-ing more each day. ___ Oh let us   love one an-oth-er,

A7

D7

G

Love one an-oth-er,   Learn-ing to walk in Je-sus' way.

Gracious Father, Hear Our Prayer

Frederick J. Gielow, Jr.

Arr. from Peter Ritter

1. Gra - cious Fa - ther hear our pray'r; Hear our prais - es
2. Lord we know that Thou art good; All good things come

and thanks - giv - ing; Help us trust Thy love and care,
from a - bove us; So we thank Thee for our food,

Help us strive for Christ - like liv - ing! Hear Thy chil - dren's
For our homes and those who love us. Help us kind to

loud ac - claim, Glo - ry to Thy ho - ly name!
oth - ers be, Thus to show our love for Thee!

Go . . . Tell

Matthew 28:7

Phyllis J. Warfel

Go quick - ly, go quick - ly, and tell, Go quick - ly, go quick - ly, and tell He is ris - en from the dead. He is ris - en from the dead. He is ris - en from the dead, Go, tell.

Spread the Good News

(Echo Song*)

L. K.

LaVern Karns

Spread the good news (good news, good news); Je - sus

lives (Je - sus lives). To all na - tions (na-tions, na-tions), Life He

gives (gives, gives). Let us bear this mes - sage ev-'ry pass - ing day, Sal-

va - tion to all who will trust and o - bey.

* Divide group into 3 parts.

108

We Can Reach Around the World

Ruth Gibbs Zwall

Evelyn F. Tarner

We can reach a - round the world with God's love, As we pray, as we give, and

go, We can reach a-round the world with God's love, That man-y, man-y oth-ers may

know. When we pray, and when we give, and tell the sto - ry, They will know the Sav-ior's

love is true. We can reach a-round the world for Je-sus, And oth-ers will love Him, too.

We Will Go to All the World

B. L. H.

Barbara Le Hays

We will go to all the world, Preach-ing in the name of our Lord,

Teach-ing Christ and Him cru-ci-fied, Praise His name o'er earth far and wide.

Ask-ing not for fame or re-ward, Hap-py in the love of the Lord.

He is ris-en! Al-le-lu-ia! Christ is ris'n in-deed!

Be a Missionary

P. J. W.

Phyllis J. Warfel

Be a mis-sion-ar-y for the Lord. Be a mis-sion-ar-y,

spread His Word. Ev-'ry Chris-tain has a big re-spon-si-bil-i-ty

Tell-ing all the world the gos-pel sto-ry, Be a mis-sion-ar-y

for the Lord. Be a mis-sion-ar-y, spread His Word.

TOPICAL INDEX

ALPHABETICAL INDEX